# The Night Visitors

*The Night Visitors* is a work of fiction. The characters are products of the author's fancy, and any resemblance between these ultra-fictional characters and real human beings, living or dead or trapped in between, is purely a matter of cosmic coincidence. The names of these characters as well as the names of business establishments also came out of nowhere. There is no disrespect intended. If anyone finds any part of this work objectionable, the author vows to give it consideration before deciding to leave it in.

For information about this title or to order books and/or electronic media, contact the publisher:

alisonkalenofske@aol.com

Cover and interior design by The Book Cover Whisperer: OpenBookDesign.biz

979-8-218320-75-1 Paperback
979-8-218-32650-0 eBook

1. Fiction. 2. Christmas. 3. Fantasy. 4. Mystery. 5. Humorous.

Printed in the United States of America

FIRST EDITION

Warning:
Literature can be thought-provoking.
Take this book in doses.

# The
# Night
# Visitors

A CHRISTMAS MYSTERY

TOMMY & ALISON
KALENOFSKE

I

**Y**e *Olde Candle Shop* is a name engraved on a
weather beaten shingle swinging on rusty hooks
over the front door of a most unusual store. It was also
painted on the storefront in tarnished gold, one gilded
letter meticulously stenciled in each small pane of an
imported French window. This same name is stitched
into the awning and appears in bold relief on the wrought
iron mailbox as well as on a tattered green carpet in the
doorway with a path worn down the middle. Although
time and tear have taken a toll on the artwork, someone
seems very proud of this name.

This candle store is at the end of a narrow cobble-
stone street known as Wimpole Place, a dark wind-
ing drive lined with the musty shops of merchants and
craftsmen that ends at the front door of the candle store,
or rather loops around a lamp post and goes back the

way it came. As the street is dark day or evening, the lamp on the post is always lit. There is a bronze lantern on the greyish brick façade, with a thick cream candle constantly burning, and through the frost and snowflakes on the windowpanes the halo of each showcase candle is reflected in the eyes of a Persian cat grooming herself on the windowsill. Two hearty junipers fan out in wooden planters on both sides of the doorway and more than one elderly woman with a snag in her shawl, has complained to the shopkeepers that the junipers need pruning. Apprehension sets in and the browser's first impression is that she has been deceived, mislead by an advertisement on the vary last page of her ladies magazine. Standing in the doorway clutching her pocketbook, intuition tells her to turn around and catch the next trolley to the Wax Emporium on Mayfair street, which advertises closer to the front of the magazine. It might even be a good idea to cancel her subscription entirely.

*So what makes this store so unusual? Maybe the answer waits inside.*

The bells over the door tinkle as the browser enters. A gush of heavy warm air escapes into the street. Flimsy lace curtains puff out, and burning wicks flicker nervously in the breeze as the door creaks closed on it's own volition. The Persian cat stops grooming itself and stares menacingly, as would any woman whose vanity is disturbed. The halos in her eyes turn to ornery rings of fire. It takes a moment for the senses to adjust to the frail light and the heavy odors, just long enough for certain questions to arise. Like why would a chandler keep a cat on the premises? Do mice eat candles?

Straight ahead in this diffuse light the showroom resembles the interior of an epicerie tucked away in a tiny Swiss village, a mountain grocery store smelling of cedar and pine, flowers and fruit, herbs and spices, evergreen and wine. Aromas seep into the hardwood floors and overhead beams where copper chandeliers hold pale yellow candles, and the taller customers are treated to a fragrance of citrus blossoms. Rows of baskets line the main isle, oriental baskets, wicker baskets, hanging baskets brimming with apricots, blueberries, wild cherries, perfumed raspberries, cornucopias wafting of fruits too exotic to be eaten.

At the end of the isle is a cluster of bushel baskets full of peaches, oranges, apples, pumpkins, and watermelons, baby ones of course. These are basic flavors a farmer or even a hunter could identify in the dark. As in most matters of perception a woman has a more sensitive sense of smell than a man, or maybe a more refined sense. A farmer can smell a change in the weather, can smell a storm coming or a dry spell. A fisherman can smell land from fifty miles at sea. A businessman can smell a deal, a gambler can smell a sure thing, but ask a man to distinguish a lavender from a lilac, and he's lost, confused, whereas the browser can do it in the dark or the halflight in this showroom designed by an eccentric candlemaker who apparently doesn't yet believe in electricity. (Inhale...exhale. Ah, much better) Sconces instead of lamps protrude from the walls on both sides of the room, scented candles instead of lightbulbs stand in the fixtures. The sconces could be silver or polished pewter, observes the browser, but there is no mistaking the scents, lavender to the left lilacs to the right. Until her vision clears she follows her nose.

Fragrances are said to be therapeutic. Sweetness aside the oil distilled from roses is said to relieve anxiety. Peppermint oil is said to cure nausea, jasmine oil eases depression, basil calms the nerves, chamomile cures insomnia, rosemary enhances the memory, clary sage induces clear and colorful dreams and the oil distilled from orange blossoms stimulates the mind body and spirit. The nose is the channel to the psyche or so it said in the advertisement in the ladies magazine, so it must be true.

Succulence drips from every corner of this illusory marketplace. The nostrils are tantalized and the mouth almost waters as one wades through tons of produce picked from fabulous groves and gardens, artificial appetizers with wicks for stems and wax for pulp. No pits, no bruises, no worms, much too perfect and much too sweet to be mistaken for genuine edibles. Still like a shopper at a fruit stand, this whimsical customer picks them up, smells them, squeezes them, sets them back down and strolls around in a dilemma while she makes up her mind whether its pie or gelatin for dessert tonight. Shipping crates laden with nutmeg, vanilla, ginger, mint sprigs and cinnamon sticks bring a variety of aperitifs to mind, followed by ice cream and mousse, or soufflés and crepes...flambé.

Still led by the nose the browser is lured across the isle by candles scented with stronger more potent aromas. She leans over diminutive barrels to sample bouquets of blackberry brandy and island rum, absinthe and maraschino, crème de menthe, coconut and strawberry schnapps, passing each candle under her nose like a snifter. These synthetic drams have a soothing influence even on a temperate browser. With the fruit baskets, spice crates, and rum barrels, one is reminded of a tropical harbor. Like a sailor on The Bounty one is almost tempted to stay. However, she does have a shopping list to fill, which brought her to this obscure street in the first place. She came here looking for a gift for someone hard to please.

Leaving the lowlands behind she finds herself in the highlands once more. She bumps into a work table cluttered with tapered candles and plastic leaves and berries, an assortment of half made centerpieces partially arranged in nosegays reminiscent of the wilds. Lilies of the valley, evergreens and heather, mountain roses, edelweiss. Even the empty vials of fragrant oils exude refreshing whiffs of winter.

By now her eyes are fully adapted to the shadowy décor. She adjusts her bifocals and details come into focus, miniscule things such as price tags and stickers. "Oh my!" She recoils at the price of everything, the drams, the fruit. Just as art imitates life, wax gives the illusion of reality, and naturally costs more.

"Would you like a cup of Tea?" The browser leaps! "I didn't mean to disturb you." added Mrs. Clover the saleslady. "A cup of tea would be nice...anytime but today. I'm in a genuine rush to find a present for my mother. She is an avid collector and especially a candle collector. Do you have any on sale?" "Right back there" said the saleslady pointing to a series of shelves at the back of the store.

The seasonal wares were stored in plain sight. When a new season rolled around the appropriate candles were slid to the front and the prices were boosted on everything but Turkeys. Turkeys were multi-seasonal so their price remained the same. There were tiny animal candles smelling like fashion models all rougey and perfumey even the skunks, not like their real life counterparts. Against the back wall stood a makeshift staircase leading naturally to nowhere. Back here the out of season goods were stored along with salvage goods with flaws, damages in shipping, an elephant with a broken trunk, a melted teddy bear and several Venus De Milos (with arms). In addition sooner or later all shopkeepers make the same mistake overstocking merchandise that for some incomprehensible reason just doesn't sell, mummies, billiard balls, rattlesnakes and so can be had for next to nothing.

While she continued her search the bells over the door tinkled again and a bevy of nuns entered the shop. "Is our Christmas votive candle order ready?" they asked Mrs. Clover who handed them a box replying " my husband makes these candles himself from beeswax, so as they burn the smell of honey will fill the air." " St Bernard would be pleased." said one of the nuns, not referring to the cloister's pet dog but to St Bernard of Clairvaux who was widely reputed to be the patron saint of candlemakers. In days past money was the source of most evil and the bazaar was the gateway to hell, the devil's minions disguised as hawkers and peddlers of goods. Women and children were warned off the marketplace and men were drawn to it. There was corruption on every corner, cutpurses, gamblers, moneylenders, liquor and after the sun went down a robber in every niche. As time went on the clergy became more lenient and it wasn't long before every guild had a patron Saint overseeing it's prosperity. After all one had to squander that accursed gold somewhere. Only Pharaohs could take it with them.

One of the nuns asked "We have a coupon from a magazine can we use it?" They hadn't read the coupon thinking it was for a discount. "No discount needed, we always donate these candles to the Church, but this coupon states you are entitled to three free kisses with every order." replied Mrs. Clover. They took the kisses giggling thinking they were a sweet snack but like everything else in this shop they were made of wax. The nuns left forgetting their kisses and one snagged her habit on the Junipers just outside the door. The browser moved toward the door also, fully intending to leave. "Wait," said Mrs. Clover. "It just came to me. What size hat do you wear? I have a solution for you. Let me call my husband, he'll be able to help." Strange question thought the browser, this is a candle shop and there was no millinery anywhere in sight.

Five steps down and five feet back from the showroom floor a door opened revealing a workshop from which Mr. Clover entered. Together the Clovers look like characters from a storybook. The wife with her rolled white hair and smiling blue eyes, eyewear on the bridge of her upturned nose, primrose cheeks, hands folded at the waist of her floral apron. Plump and pretty as a cookie jar. Her husband with his long white hair and whiskers, shaggy eyebrows, baggy pants, as stout and cuddly as Geppetto. Seeing them side by side its hard to imagine them in any other business.

Shortly after the nuns left, Chrissy Parlett the landlady entered the shop after having parked her little electric car next to the lamp post. "Ms. Parlett, how nice to see you. Mrs. Clover gestured "You know my husband, the finest chandler in the business. Chandler is English for candlemaker. And how are you this evening?" Chrissy responded " I was barely able to arrive here. There is a flood of water at the entrance to your street which I will have to see about having fixed as soon as possible. I'm here to do some last minute Christmas shopping and also the rental letter for the new year. Mr. Gatewood has me delivering them." " Mr. Gatewood seems like such a nice young man." Offered Mr. Clover. " So did Doctor Jekyll!" responded Chrissy. "Please have some tea." Mrs. Clover handed her a cup. "You will feel refreshed and better able to make some nice gift selections once you can fully appreciate the quality items in our shop." Why do the English always feel that a cup of tea solves everything thought Chrissy taking a few sips and finding herself actually calming down.

II

*P**OOM!* A burner explodes in the back room blowing
the workshop door open again and jolting Chrissy
back to reality. "Tricky things those burners" apologized
Mr. Clover. Fumes! Not microspores but heavy lumber-
ing clouds of sweetness rolled through the doorway, thick
syrupy vaporballs shot through with flying chunks of
blistery wax. "It's all part of my new creation" smiled
Mr. Clover. He seemed a little edgy and unsure but Mrs.
Clover prompted him to reenter the workshop. Shortly
after he emerged backward, pushing the door with his
rump, then turned around carrying a heavy tray, taking babysteps like a first day pubmaid. There was a
large square object in the middle of the tray concealed
by a velvet covercloth. He set the end of the tray on
the counter and slid it forward ever so gently. Taking
a breath he lifted the velvet. Underneath was a silver

inlaid box akin to a jewel box, where one might store a family treasure, a tiara or Faberge Egg.

"Give me your honest opinion, have you ever seen anything like this?" He had a certain gleam in his eyes, a look of anticipation an artist reserves for peers instead of laymen. He flipped the latch releasing the collapsible sides.

"My goodness! "Uttered the browser. "It's a head!!!!" "I didn't mean to startle you, what I mean is I did mean to startle you but perhaps I brought out the wrong head?" "The wrong head?" Chrissy asked. "How can you have the wrong head. You mean you have more in there?" "Yes lots of them. We're having a big promotion for them next week. We plan to fill the entire display window. So what do you think?" "I think you are a lunatic! Goodbye!" uttered the Browser edging toward the door.

Fatigue is magician, a sleight of mind artist pulling birds out of his hat at the most gullible hours just like now. The magician is on a roll and that makes anything seem possible no matter how absurd. The browser is drowsy and susceptible to inner and outer influences. "Please open your eyes and look more closely" urged Mrs. Clover gently. Slowly the browser peeked out of one eye then opened the other. "Amazing, impossible, fantastic. It's meeeee!!!!"

And it was. An almost perfect replica, a portrait of

her head cast in wax with a wick strategically disguised as an errant hair. Mr. Clover had fashioned it while she had strolled about the shop. "But the nose is slightly crooked" she commented. Mr. Clover picked up a pair of plyers and a hammer "Just a minor adjustment here…" as he performed a bit of rhinoplasty, on the candle of course. He pulled the nose right off the face repositioned it and pressed it back into the warm wax. However the cheeks and lips were now too puffy. Also one of the ears was lower than the other. He peeled off the left ear and reapplied it a half an inch higher. With expert even pressure he pushed and prodded until he had restored the balance and the head was complete. The browser was breathless as if the entire operation had been preformed directly on her. "Do you like it?" asked Mrs. Clover. "You don't have to buy just give us your opinion. It's an experiment."

Honestly and surprisingly the revised version suited her better than his first try. The face staring back at her appeared much more youthful, small lines and crowsfeet all but gone, similar to portraits of monarchs and presidents on coins and paper bills. Her somewhat lightheaded opinion is that this finest chandler in the business has outdone himself. Some magic is at work here. Along with her older skin he seems to have peeled back the hands of time. This wizard of a candlemaker has captured a moment from her past, so warm and tender that she even remembers what she was thinking at that exact moment. It was the first night of her second honeymoon sitting across from her husband ruminating over the dessert menu thinking Cherries Jubilee or Torte Cherise? It was then her husband raised his Kirsch to the first night of their first honeymoon and gave her a Cherub necklace and another verse to the composition he began on their wedding day. He gave her a new verse every year, his goal being an epic love poem. He called it Pour Mon Cheri. Not totally original but it's the thought that one cherishes.

Two heads are better than one when solving life's sundry problems. "And you said you have more? Do you have one of me?" asked Chrissy Parlett hoping he did. "Oh yes and you will recognize many of the subjects. We did them from photographs. You'll not find these at the Wax Emporium" ( One of their blander competitors.) spoke a proud Mr. Clover. He went back into the workshop and returned with a candle head of Parlett and also one of Medusa which had wicks for each tongue of the 20 snakes on her head. "Which one is me?" asked Chrissy laughing knowing that some of her employees thought of her in these mythical terms.

The browser had made her decision. "Not only do I like my candle I will take it!" and after paying left the store in a much better mood knowing her present would be well received.

NEXT DOOR WAS A sign that said Treasures from a Dark Continent. Another stop wouldn't hurt so she decided to visit. Shopping for genuine collectibles had evolved into a serious quest for her, combing junk shops, and esoteric candle stores year after year, prowling estate auctions and rummage sales, chasing down false claims and bogus advertisements. Last year the browser had traveled partway across Europe for a candlestick once owned by a Roman Centurion only to find out it was made in Egypt. It even said so on the bottom: Made in Egypt.

Appropriately as she entered and walked over the crunchy sounding floor, there was almost total darkness, but enough light to see that the walls and shelves were lined with primitive jewelry, amulets, rugs, pottery, shrunken heads (which she hoped were imitations like her candle), and several magic lamps ready for rubbing. She passed a wall of primitive masks that would wet a modern artists palette made from polished wood and animal hair. On an upturned crate near the wall she spied a mysterious brown bottle. She moved closer. It stood two feet high in the dust where it may have been standing for years like a bottle of vintage Claret. By the weight she knew there was something inside. It appeared to be a Genie, a fetching one too, as jubilant as a sultan, with golden earrings, ankle bracelets, a silver necklace and a huge pink pearl nestling on his slippery belly.

His luminous green eyes were pointed heavenward and his hands were clasped to his chest but it's not like he is praying more like he is responding to applause, praise for some feat just performed. She tapped on the bottle to see if he moved. Of course he doesn't, but its fun to think that he might. Looking through the bottle she sees the artist's name ymmot. She is overjoyed, this appears to be an original collectible. There is a price tag strung around the stopper. If the price is fair, and even if the price is outlandish, at this point she doesn't care, she has to have it. She flipped the tag over and here is what it says in big red letters. SOLD! "Drat!" Sometimes ladies do swear. Like a drunkard in the pantry she has one vain hope that maybe there is another bottle to be found around here somewhere.

"Hello? Is anybody here? Where is a pushy clerk when you need one! Can somebody help me?" A shadowy figure with his back to her was sweeping up. He turned and she saw that he wore long embroidered robes and a witch doctor mask. He had rings on every finger and earrings the size of ancient coins stamped with the faces of one eyed emperors. His necklace looked to be strung with uncut rubies and emeralds. Around the walls lined with mirrors his garb and complexion appeared to change as he moved towards her. This proprietor certainly fit the part she thought a little nervously at this point. The entire shop sent chills up her chakras. To tarry or to flee she wonders. Swapping his broomstick for a spear he turned up the light and she noticed that he had several jars of exotic dust on his counter as well as a sign that read Free Bag of Walnuts With Every Purchase. Two monkeys, tails entwined each with a bag of walnuts were snacking away and throwing the walnut shells on the floor faster than they could be swept up. "I am Mr. Obujati, how may I help?" he asked. She approached the counter stepping over a Gnu rug almost getting her tippet caught on the horns that were still intact. "The item I really like appears to be sold. Do you have more genies?" He shook his head. "Everything in the shop except the two monkeys are one of a kind." It was for the best as the listed price was not only outlandish but outrageous. "However I can contact you if the current purchasers change their mind." " Thank you please do." With that she left, knowing that at the very least her head candle should be more than an adequate present.

BACK AT THE CANDLE shop without any customers there to listen in, Chrissy was yearning to know how Mr. Clover did these unique portraits. "How do you create these candles so quickly?" " Ah that's my secret." "It will be safe with me." She offered. "And even safer remaining with me." However as with many artistes pride and his desire for recognition finally overcame secrecy and Mr. Clover led her down into the workshop. Her boots stuck to the wax as she descended the stairway. To the side one slightly blue daddylonglegs scurried up his slightly green waxy web. There were splotches of color on the bricks where wax had cooled and hardened and had been scraped off, just recently. From the looks of things these explosions appear routine. There on the shelves were jars marked Noses, Chins, Ears, Lips. "So this is your workshop?" said Chrissy. "it looks more like a snackbar for cannibals." "It's simple really" said Clover. "I have all these parts that I premade along with heads of standard shapes and sizes. No two people have exactly the same head but I can arrange them into a close approximation of almost anyone by gently heating all the appropriate component parts softening them and then I can apply them all within twenty minutes. Now that you know my secret I feel I can trust you not to reveal it." "I would never do that" Chrissy said "but I urge you to get this patented right away."

WITH ONE LAST LOOK around the candle shop Chrissy proceeded to the counter and in a wooden box next to the cash register, packed in shredded newspaper were a dozen earthenware shakers glazed with leaves, vines and tiny red flowerbuds. The wording on the box was in a foreign language. "I'm not sure what that says but would you like one we are almost out." said Mrs. Clover. Almost out indeed! thought Parlett. A shopkeepers ploy, and if I came back tomorrow there will be crates of exotic dust piled to the rafters. Still it can't hurt. She picked one up and some of the dust stuck to her hand as she handed it to Mrs. Clover to wrap.

A dog or was it a wolf howled in the distance as a London Bobbie strolled by the shop twirling his nightstick. Since the fog was rolling in it made him a little hard to see. Normally he would drop in for tea and pleasant conversation but it was getting later so he only waved and the Clovers and Chrissy waved back through the window.

CHRISSY'S LAST STOP ON Wimpole place was next door at the same Treasures from a Dark Continent that the browser had just left. When she entered Obujati was sitting in a chief's chair smoking a Kuba pipe and studying a chessboard introspectively sipping something from a gourd. Carefully stepping over a mechanical crocodile with glowing red eyes circling the live monkeys she approached him. "Starting the celebrations early I see." He blew out a smoke ring that fluttered precariously then encircled the head of a Zulu club. "Just brushing up on my game and this is a non alcoholic drink" he replied. He removed his mask. "Don't be alarmed it's just a fertility mask. I have a date with destiny tonight." "Is my order ready?" she asked as she handed him his rental letter. He took out a small box. "One paperweight" (An englassed Tarantula.) "It's beautiful, my son will love it. Thanks again"

OUTSIDE THE FOG WAS now as thick as Baskerville moor so that driving with limited visibility she almost ran over the browser. "Can I give you a lift?" she asked. "Oh thank you." Women are enchanted by fog, or lost in it. Fog is good cover for all sorts of mischief. A foggy night is darkness with a twist of intrigue. Tonight the fog is changing colors going from a misty grey to a dusty green like the sky before a tornado, just before the funnel appears, and getting thicker by the moment.

They chugged along slowly and silently in her little electric car, towards the end of Wimpole place. The flood from earlier was gone now and the street was dry, so the pipes must have been repaired already. That was quick thought Chrissy, thankful that she didn't have to plow though water on her way out. They proceeded to the tunnel just ahead, a short passageway and like going through a time portal they entered into Raspberry Hill Mall, the World's largest shopping mall.

# III

*The Mall management* office was not listed on the Mall directory and there were no signs directing you. The only way to find it was to go to the information desk, identify yourself and your appointment time and state your business. Don't bother asking for a guide because the guide would just guide you to the information desk. And nevermind asking a security guard because to them it was like asking to get to the President. Don't be surprised if you find yourself being frisked and scanned, and then taken to the information desk.

The office was situated on the tenth floor, right in the middle, dead center, in the thick of it in any direction. "Good Morning." Flora, the mall Secretary always greeted everyone. She had a schoolteacherish patience and appeared to know everything going on in the mall. Gatewood had brought Flora a flower. He had given the florist a dollar tip as he always tipped but never paid for an item. The flower actually cost three dollars but shorting everyone or expecting it free was his usual way of emphasizing his importance. Gatewood was cheap, he believed that a penny saved was a penny earned. True, but the problem was that he had never even earned a penny ever so it was all about cutting back to get ahead, which in reality puts you behind.

Flora was immune to pressure of any kind. She reacted to hubbub like a schoolmarm nursing a sarsaparilla in the middle of a bar fight. She could operate two computers, a switchboard, three telephones, a videophone hotline, greet all visitors, register all complaints from tenants and shoppers and order the week's coffee while knitting a monogramed sweater for her granddaughter's puppy. She also had a gift for small talk, a talent not everyone possesses, lightweight conversation she laced with subliminal advertising. "It's a bit chilly out there today, you should have worn a scarf young man. They have some handsome ones over at *Gentleman's Apparel* that you could have gifted to yourself. And what is your schedule for today Mr. Gatewood?" "I think I'll be at Putter's Island all day making sure everything is working correctly." Flora responded with "You never worked a day in your life, so what made you decide to start now?"

Gatewood was the assistant mall manager and

Macintosh's nephew and never let anyone forget it since Macintosh was the Mall's owner and creator. "If you're gonna start you might as well start at the top." No one knew Macintosh's net worth which was by any standards, A LOT. This mall would never have any financial worries because as most billionaires have their pet projects this was Macintosh's. The shopkeepers here didn't have to follow company policies because there were no policies and they were encouraged to improvise. Macintosh was very elusive, didn't do interviews and had never been seen on camera making him a prime target for investigative reporters and roving photographers who had never been able to quite pin down his whereabouts. Even this morning there were a couple of them loitering around half expecting to see him on this important day of the year. Not a chance.

Macintosh's vision was to promote hundreds of small and unique shops with items you could not find anywhere else. He helped the entrepreneurs get set up and if they were successful he then helped them to expand their business horizons. In case anyone in the future tried to build nearby the mall he had purchased additional adjacent acreage and sold the air rights to himself so that he could expand outward and upward whenever necessary to maintain the integrity of his designs. He had situated the mall far enough away from the nearest town and airport so that cab drivers could make money

ferrying the customers to the location while acting as
unofficial tour guides while they drove their passengers
over since most cabbies love to chit chat.

Macintosh believed in Atmosphere. Anyone who
had lived long enough remembers what atmosphere
is, remembers the texture, what it looks like, what it
feels like, what it smells like. The corner saloon had
atmosphere, the grocery store, the old library, the old
church, the old schoolhouse before they tore it down.
The musky odor of the moose head in grandfather's den
smacked of atmosphere. The sheet music on the piano
in grandmother's parlor, as well as the sunporch of the
widow next door and her potted plants when she invited
you for lemonade after you finished raking her lawn.
Atmosphere goes back to other days like a scrapbook
or an old postcard. It goes back to an era of mahogany and marble, etched mirrors, brass railings and real
leather upholstery. It was a time of small business when
grocers, druggists, barbers, florists and even musicians
lived right on the premises. Atmosphere was personal,
it came from the heart, came from pride, came from
heritage. It changed neighborhood by neighborhood,
district by district, from snob hill to the wharves. No
two shops, offices, department stores, restaurants or
banks were alike. It was something genuine. It could
not be falsified or manufactured, although here at the
mall it had been lovingly reconstructed, almost, not

quite, but close enough. Atmosphere could be ornate or shabby, It could be spic and span as a hotel lobby or as dingy as a wine cellar. Yet no matter where, it always had a lasting vitality that stayed behind even after the occupants had moved on, so strong or gentle was their influence. Here there were no big box stores, Raspberry Hill was the big box that all the little boxes came in.

Gatewood didn't share that vision. His vision was that large corporate stores were the only way to go like at other big malls. Sure, a few unique stores would be ok but he didn't see much sense in them profitwise. This is why Macintosh had hired Chrissy Archer to be the mall manager. She ran a comfortable ship and took Japanese Management one step further, Female Japanese Management. She had a reputation of being a people person and spent much of her day visiting and checking on the various shops and stores to their betterment. She loved her job, not for the expansive salary but because she believed in Macintosh's vision and the satisfaction of helping their tenants' businesses grow and thrive.

One of the unwritten rules in business was to be wary of working for a family owned company unless you were a member of the family, because when it comes to a confrontation the family member, no matter how incompetent, usually always wins. Nepotism was like walking on glass, hard to know how to deal with the boss's relative. The showdown was long overdue. Traditionally women in business use their maiden names while at work, it was how they kept their identities separate. Mrs. Chrissy Archer or Ms. Chrissy Parlett, her business name, wasn't too worried because her husband Chick, a TV reporter, was already earning enough to support their little family regardless of the ultimate outcome.

EARLIER THAT MORNING CHRISSY was rushing around getting ready. "Come on kids I'm in a hurry." "What about our breakfast Mom?" "Finish your cereal and we'll have a proper meal at the mall. Looks like you are coming to work with me until Grandma arrives." They hadn't been to the mall yet. They lived somewhat sheltered lives. Their world consisted of at home with each other or at school with a few school friends.

Chrissy's husband Chick stacked the papers he was working on, replaced the hood on his *1969 Olivetti Valentine* and wandered into the room. "Why don't you do yourself a favor and buy a computer?" Chrissy asked for the umpteenth time. Unphased Chick responded "you know I prefer this typewriter. The words seem to be more authentic somehow besides it's very portable and doesn't need electricity." Chrissy made a mental note to purchase him a laptop while shopping today as the constant clickety clack of the keys late at night when he was working on a story often kept her awake. Chick finished his coffee and the English Muffin with

Cashew butter and Cinnamon he toasted himself daily. His morning snack also included one more tidbit which he kept on top of the cupboard out of reach of the children. But it wasn't there today.

"If you're looking for your cigarette" said Chrissy "I threw it away." Downcast he responded "I just wanted to hold it for a minute." Chick was attending non smoking support groups but it wasn't working too well. He was trying everything and even carried a couple of packs of Red Hots to help quell the cravings. A part of his failure was his philosophy. "It's an occupational hazard. Did you ever see a top notch reporter without a cigarette like in the movies?"

"Well it hasn't enhanced your reporting. Who can forget your ridiculous story about the Frisbee catching duck." "Well how about the *Fuzzy Zombies*, that one wasn't too bad." Chick had filmed a story about a retired taxidermist and his wife a retired roboticist who had combined their skills into a very interesting cottage industry the reanimation of deceased pets. Chick and his camera crew followed the entire process from the initial skinning, quite bloody, to the insertion of the animatronic metal endoskeleton, witnessing the reanimation of a beloved hunting dog. "What kind of dog is this?" "An Irish Water Spaniel." "What happened to him?" "He drowned." A *Fuzzy Zombie* was the perfect gift for a heartbroken pet owner. The proof was in the eyes of the bereaved duck hunter when he saw his long time companion wagging his tail and prancing up the walk with a mallard in his mouth. However, the powers that be at the station decided that this was in bad taste and not something the viewers would want to watch while eating during the dinner hour, so instead they ran a segment about stocking stuffers and then cut to a commercial for *Creepy Crawlies Pest & Roach Control & Bug Spray.*

"The best one of all was Lanky the giraffes' zoo birth. I think I can still see the little scar where Lanky's mother bit you." " It's true," he conceded, "all my stories are ridiculous but it wont always be that way." Chick had one story that burned a hole in his back pocket. He had actually met Macintosh at a company staff party and chatted with him about his background and his vision of the mall and what that entailed. This was the ultimate conundrum. If he wrote that story it would elevate him into the national spotlight. It would however destroy his marriage with Chrissy as this ultimate betrayal would never be forgiven by her. His ambition waged war with his loyalty. Do nice guys finish last he pondered? No, he decided they usually end up somewhere in the middle with a clear conscience able to sleep at night. So fortunately loyalty and love always won and he resigned himself to finding another great story. There had to be one out there somewhere.

Kacy, their daughter, keeps wandering off. A scream came from the playroom, a little girl's scream. But there was no need to panic. This happened ten times a day. It was just her brother picking on her, Kacy came stomping out of the room. "Mom, I want a new brother." "What's wrong with the one you have honey?" "I hate him."

Five minutes later they were bosom buddies again. At their ages it's brother and sister against the world. Sibling bonding is a beautiful thing. They ran hot and cold on each other, it was a love-hate relationship minute to minute. They didn't know it yet but they would never be closer than they were right now.

Ten minutes after that. "Not again what did he do now?" "He kicked my dog across the room!" (Stuffed animals). "Why did he do that?" "Because I beat him at the video game." "Why don't you let him win once in a while?" "What for, he beats me at everything else. Can we get a real dog?" "Dad, can I stay up and wait for Santa tonight. I need him to bring me something." "What do you need?" he asked. She whispered in Chick's ear. "What's wrong with the one you have?" "He's a monster!" Endearingly, " I think you're both a couple of monsters."

Kacy believed in Santa, and many other childhood beliefs. So when the Groundhog didn't see his shadow she cried. Even worse her Grandma had taken her to see the play *Peter Pan*, so Kacy also believed in fairies which was the only way to keep Tinkerbell alive. As children both Chrissy and Chick had performed in that play in school. Chrissy had played Wendy and Chick was a most admirable crocodile. Peter Pan is traditionally always played by a girl and ironically their Peter Pan has fulfilled her destiny and is now a Colonel in the Air Force.

Jody being a couple of years older than his little sister was quite skeptical about everything. This was further fueled by emulating his dad and acting like a reporter. "Do you see all those presents under the tree. If Santa doesn't arrive until midnight then how did all those presents get here?" "Mom and Dad put them there and I even helped." " So you admit that Santa didn't put them there." "You're so dumb. Haven't you figured it out yet. Santa gives us the most important presents, the ones that we ask for in our Santa letters, and mom and dad give us the rest, the socks and mittens and the Treasury bills for college." Jody took out a tape measure. " How does Santa with a waist that big fit through this small hole?" he said measuring the fireplace flu. "Simple, I asked Dad and he said that he let him in through the patio." "I suppose you wrote Santa a letter." said Jody realizing he was getting no where with that line of questioning. "Yes I did and last year I got most of what I wanted except for the pony." " Do you think you will get a pony this year?" "I didn't ask for a pony this year, I just asked for a horseback ride."

On the phone Chrissy tells her mother to get the key at the front desk of the hotel so she could drop off her luggage at their apartment when she arrived. "Chick has to work so I'll have the kids meet you at a restaurant in the Mall around 1 pm. It's called *The Treehouse*. It's right next to a huge Christmas tree, you cant miss it." "Can't you call the sitter?" "She went to Las Vegas for the holidays." "Your sitter went to Vegas? Are you sure that you aren't paying her too much?

.

# IV

*National Parks* often have their own radio channel to relay instructions for ingress and egress. Taking a cue from this, Raspberry Hill had it's own radio frequency. There were scintillating signs at every onramp. You are now entering the Raspberry Hill complex. Turn your dial all the way to the left and follow along with suggestions. Once tuned in the static congealed into a deep coaxing voice. Remember the point of entrance, remember where you came in. Plan to spend some memorable time. If you are already here then you are more than welcome. For those of you that have been here before don't be in such a hurry this time around. You are guaranteed to see sights and wonders that you missed. Consult your brochure.

Outside the mall, the promenade leading to the main entrance was lined with two rows of twenty foot raspberry trees. In reality there were no such things as raspberry trees, everyone knows raspberries grew on bushes. Here raspberries grew on trees, vines, and on their own like tulips. At night the trees lit up. There was a giant raspberry speaking a jolly greeting in nineteen languages including Mandarin. Because seventyfive percent of all shoppers were women the raspberry had a male voice. It sounded poetic but with a sense of humor, sensitive but secure in it's masculinity, it was great with kids, had an eye for bargains and it was a good listener.

As Frank Lloyd Wright had said ...a building that is ugly by day will, if illuminated, be ugly by night as well... From the outside most malls looked like prisons. This mall looked as fantastic from the outside as it did inside, day or night. The entire exterior façade resembled a giant luxury hotel or an exclusive ivy league college and the entrances mirrored those of mansions. The finest materials had been used including wood, natural stones. granite and marble most unexpected in a shopping destination. The mall didn't yet qualify as a wonder of the world but perhaps a national park or at least a national monument and Macintosh was working on it. This wasn't the Grand Canyon or Niagara Falls, but it was a lot more fun. He had tossed around hundred's of names – Something Supermall, something, something Supercenter. The Mall of something, something. Each one as flat and colorless as the next. There was the idea of naming it after one of the animals the state was renowned for, but the most famous animals here were poisonous. (Though Rattlesnake Mall had a certain ring to it.)

Marketing experts considered a name-the-mall contest, having the public submit names like they do for name changes for baseball and football teams. But they decided against it in the end, fearing the nine hundred ninety nine thousand nine hundred and ninety nine rejectees would be insulted and never shop here. As a jest the local TV 5 station had viewers vote on a list of possible names. Coming in at number one was The Great Big Mall on the Hill. That said it all. At number nine Killer Bee Mall named for the many swarms increasingly seen in the area. At number ten Let's pray There's never a Mudslide Mall. Finally it was Macintosh himself who did the christening. The fax was concise and to the point as was his style. *Raspberry Hill Mall*, Case closed.

Tourist attractions are often disappointingly smaller or less impressive than one was led to believe. "What? That's it?" Examples were The Alamo, The Tower of Pisa, The London bridge at Lake Havasu. To preempt this Macintosh had invented a system called Reverse Promo. In the ads they made the mall look smaller than it actually was. That way when people showed up they were completely blown away. The first indoor shopping mall was built in 1956 in Southdale Minnesota and with modifications is still fully functioning today although mostly locals visited there now. People travel from everywhere to see Mount Everest, The Great Wall of China or the Pyramids. Chrissy found it amazing how far people were willing to travel to see this new shopping mall. Apparently from all over the world. Even while Raspberry Hill was being built people would drive out just to watch the construction making it a tourist attraction even before it opened. If you were looking for new experiences this was the place. On opening day several months previous, people were camped on the grounds for over a week, making the parking lot look like an affluent hobo jungle.

Chrissy and the kids walked through the mall's employee entrance after she keyed in her secret code. A bird flew in ahead of them. Birds were attracted to the place, nobody knew why. A Basset hound scampered out of the bushes and followed them in and then hid. Stray dogs had found a home here also and the word had spread via some unknown canine communication that this was a safe place.

Once inside Chrissy found her golf cart parked outside *The Bag It* luggage store. She couldn't figure out what it was doing there until she studied their merchandise through the window. The store sold suitcases, briefcases, wallets, purses ....and golf bags. "OK kids pile into my cart and off we go." The kids were amazed at the variety of stores they passed. The lights in each store were programmed to turn on two hours before opening to give early window shoppers and mall walkers a preview of the wonderful and varied merchandise inside. "What do you do here mom?" asked Kacy. "I'm in charge of all of this." she replied. "You mean like a playground supervisor?" "Something like that." Actually she felt more like the mayor of a small city albeit appointed not voted in. Had there been a vote of her constituents though she would have been overwhelmingly voted for as she was that well liked and respected by all concerned.

When they arrived at the cookie shop, *C C & Company*, the golf cart lurched to a stop. Chrissy checked the voltmeter and it read empty. Zilch! "What!" Gatewood had borrowed her cart yesterday as he had said that his was in the repair shop for some overdue maintenance. When done with hers he had neglected to plug it back in. "That inconsiderate ..." Realizing that she couldn't totally vent as the children were with her she got out and as she was trying to push the cart, Herbie, the cookie man came out of the cookie shop with a plate of cookies for the kids. He was dressed as a round chocolate chip cookie and his eyes peered out from two chocolate chip holes. His name was Chip Chocolate and he imagined that once his store took off he would become as famous for cookies as Ronald is for burgers so working long hours for low pay was no problem. In fact the one commercial he had already made validated his career path to eventually, he envisioned, being a balloon in the yearly Thanksgiving Day Parade, even though he looked more like a giant air filled tire man than a giant cookie. He helped her push the cart, but when they reached the antique car stand he flipped over like a giant turtle. This happened a lot as his suit apparently needed some work.

A man in black slacks and a t-shirt came over to help flip Chip back right side up. They pushed the cart to the side and then he put on his cummerbund, dicky and jacket. "Thank you Mr. Pembroke." "Please call me Hopkins." 'Hopkins Pembroke. Sounds like royalty."

"Landed Gentry back in the dark ages." "What happened?" 'My ancestors were victimized by some rather uncouth real estate speculators." "Who were they?" "Vikings!"

"I've never seen a used car salesman in a Tuxedo before, why the touch of class?" "These are not used cars, Miss Parlett, they are fully registered, turn-of-the-century antiques, made in America, unretouched, in mint condition, original upholstery, original paint, original rubber and on consignment from the families of the original owners." "Little old ladies, I suppose that only drove them once a month?" "Quite correct. Every model on display is an electric car. Ladies preferred them to gas burners because they didn't have to crank them up, smell the fumes or get their outfits soaked in gasoline at the gas pumps." "Correction then, I have never seen any car salesman in a Tuxedo." "Don't let the feathers fool you. Mall tours are just a hobby with me. Back home in London I have a Honda dealership. You should see my commercials. I'm dressed as a blighter and I'm known as 'appy 'oppy the 'onda man with discounts so 'efty I'm driving myself to the poor 'ouse!" "And that works?" It works better than my original persona." "And what was that?" "A little old lady!"

"Ms. Parlett, you should drive one of these while making your rounds today. A test drive so to speak." "What is the selling price?" " Two Hundred and Twenty thousand." "How much did it cost brand new?" "Twenty two hundred, but you could write it off on your expense account. It's much classier than a golf cart. At least just drive it around for today as it would be good advertising for me and lots of fun for you and the kids." "Done!" Chrissy started to get in the car. "Wrong side madam. This automobile was manufactured in nineteen thirteen, which means the steering wheel is on the right." He opened the door and helped her into the drivers seat. "It wasn't until nineteen fourteen that your Henry Ford moved the steering column to the left side and upset the entire balance of nature."

Parlett drove off towards the office and she lectured her son as she drove. "I want you to keep a close eye on your sister today, don't let her out of your sight. Not for a minute." "Isn't that Grandma's job?" "Grandma wont be here until later and you know how your sister likes to wander off, so do me a favor and keep an eye on her." "And you young lady, you stick close to your brother. If either one of you gets lost just find a security guard, tell him who you are and the guard will come and find me. There's one right over there." She pointed as a guard rode by on horseback. "Do they all ride horses and where do they keep them?" "Not all guards ride horses, but today everyone will be wearing costumes and the many of the guards will be wearing Nutcracker soldier uniforms."

As they pressed on Parlett spied a sugarplum fairy and her thumb was out. "Get in Soozie, you will be much needed today It's your job as talent coordinator to keep all the acts you hired under control." "Some of those people scare me." " You hired them, they're your people so scare them back!" Soozie was an event planner genius but like most 'genius' she had a quirky imagination and needed to be kept in check. Once in a while Soozie slipped one past Chrissy, like the sword swallower. He was definitely a crowd pleaser but the big question was what did a man who could eat fire and swallow three swords down his throat have to do with Christmas? Nothing, but he was a big hit. Soozie had her own office complete with a mini stage so that she could audition the applicants and have them perform their acts, On her schedule for today was a man dressed as a kangaroo who was also a ventriloquist. The puppet, a small kangaroo was in the pouch which was zipped closed, Soozie had seen the video clips of his performances and had an idea that she would run past his agent. While the puppet talked the big kangaroo would reach into the pouch and pass out free samples of mall memorabilia. Children and parents alike would love it.

They drove on "What's in that little bag?" asked Chrissy "It's too small to be a purse." "It's pixie dust. The salesperson called it exotic dust but since I am a sugarplum fairy for today it's pixie dust now." They passed a clown on stilts and then a mime directing imaginary traffic. Both had their faces painted and wore costumes prompting Jody to ask "Mom what's the difference between a clown and a mime?" "Clowns serve a purpose."

After navigating around three of the seven fountains in the mall they finally reached the office. "Mom can we go by the wishing fountain again?" asked Kacy. "What for?" "So I can add to my wish." "I'm all out of quarters. Maybe Grandma can take you later."

'GOOD MORNING" GREETED FLORA "I must say you are late today. The opening bell is in an hour." Macintosh loved the stock market opening bell and had installed his own bells which played a new tune each day to open the mall. "Unavoidable. And I know it's going to be a very busy day but Flora I will need to have my children here today until their grandmother arrives." Flora handed Parlett a stack of official looking letters. "Mr. Gatewood needs you to hand out these rent letters today." "Isn't that his job?" "He said he has never been able to ask for money." Flora rolled her eyes. "Well we certainly have our work cut out for us today" said Chrissy. "Better than not having any work cut out for us." Flora had a talent for bringing everyone back to reality.

" Honey you need to hire an assistant, a real one with talent and brains, the usual qualifications. Oh and the dog catcher is here to round up all the stray dogs in the mall. Sometimes a professional is needed!" Parlett was straightforward in a roundabout way. She stated emphatically "Well tell him that he must wait until after closing to start. We don't want him chasing after them through today's crowds, it's a safety concern and bad PR. Also call security and tell them to expect him this evening and that he needs a pass." The dog catcher preferred Animal Control Specialist which allowed him to round up cats, mice and birds also, although lately there were no mice. Apparently the two Barn Owls that had taken up residence had solved that problem nature's way.

As Soozie headed to her office she called back to Parlett, "Don't forget your costume." Parlett entered the wardrobe room and picked out a Nineteen hundred's little old lady costume. "I might as well have a costume to match my car." she mused.

V

*Christmas Eve* the mall opened early at 6 am. First the lights went low simulating a solar eclipse. Flashing lasers piercing the semi darkness followed by holographic pyrotechnics which commenced a light show of changing colors just like the real northern lights. Banners unfurled accompanied by bagpipes sounding more like bassoons, a more pleasant sound, and logo balloons looking like two thousand raspberries descended as the skylit dome above opened. After some oohing and aahing by the crowd they were snapped up as souvenirs. A parade of the toy soldier drill team marched around accompanied by music emanating from Macintosh's bell signaling that the stores were now open for business!

It was a breathtaking sight. The mall was fully decorated with all manner of Yuletide decorations including forty Christmas trees spread out over all twenty floors. There were giant snow globes in a constant state of agitation with the snow swirling and never settling simulating enclosed blizzards not unlike the real blizzard that was on it's way that very day. Thrilled shoppers marveled at all the activity. The crowd was even bigger than expected due to the news report about the incoming snowstorm and so everyone wanted to complete their shopping and get on home while it was still clear. As a bonus it was also Small Business Saturday which featured just the type of unique shops that Macintosh promoted for the mall.

Soozie had positioned continuous events on all floors, including jugglers, acrobats and carolers. There were The Tapdancng Santas (which were two St Nick's doing the Nickolas Brothers), fashion shows, craft shows, high wire artists and barber shop quartets "How much do they charge?" "Nothing. They pass the hat, then donate the money to charity." "Book em", strangely there were no beauty shop quartets, Also there were Town Cryers "OYea, OYea, OYea," and a puppet show. For some reason the puppet show was closed. Parlett knew why. Scipio, the puppeteer started imbibing early in the day and gradually sobered up to be completely clear headed when it came time to secure his valuable puppets for the evening performance only to regress again once the show was completed.

If the shoppers got hungry, there were four food

courts providing the usual faire and for the more adventurous, side streets with fanciful names fanned out like the spokes of a wheel. There you could sample national cuisines from around the world. The food areas featured robot servers and robot cleaneruppers as well as talking trash cans directing patrons where to stash their trash. All the food courts featured live trees to give the feeling of dining in a park. (But without the flies.) Macintosh had thought of everything and Parlett was there for anything he might have overlooked. The mall had it's own mailmen, as the Post Office had no choice but to open a branch inside the mall and it was busier than the main branch downtown. The mall also had it's own unbribable health inspector and two paperboys. There was a Dental office, a mini-ER in case of emergencies, For Eyes, the optometrist and eyewear store, several prize winning hair and nail salons, an art gallery featuring Macintosh's prized art collection in rotation and even a barber shop (without a quartet).

SOOZIE'S PREMIERE EVENT OF the day was about to start. An Interview with Santa Claus. Not wanting to drag the kids with her on her rounds to the shops, Parlett dropped them off at the interview location knowing that at least Kacy would enjoy it. "For after the interview here is a bag of change and you can both go and play video games at the arcade right over there. At 1pm you can meet

Grandma at The Treehouse restaurant next to The Tree so be good and no shenanigans." "What's a shenanigan?" Kacy whispered. Jody shrugged. "Don't know."

At the very center of the mall there was a flat round stage, which was used for concerts, gatherings and special events. When not in use the stage opened, the cover retracted and the mall's largest fountain would activate. The water would shoot up all twenty floors bouncing off the dome at the top like a multicolored coffee percolator and was accompanied by a changing musical selection. On clear days the dome would open and the water would shoot right through for another fifty feet and could be seen for miles. Today the cover was now closed and on the stage rows of chairs were filled with excited patrons awaiting the big event.

Soozie was bubbling over as she introduced "Parents and children the man of the hour. Santa". This Santa was a media darling, a radiant butterball with a silver tongue. His real name was Snake but people were always telling him he looked like Santa Claus, the original Santa Claus of the 1930's Cola ads. He had two choices, shave, get a haircut and a regular job, or capitalize on the resemblance. He liked to travel and Santa could get a job anywhere in the world he reasoned. Then he went to Santa School and graduated at the top of his class. He started working out of his garage with a second-hand sewing machine and built his empire from there dispelling rumors that everything was made in China. (It's one of the dream stories in America as thousands of fortunes have sprouted in garages).

Soozie hushed the crowd and the interview began.

Q "Why are you wearing sunglasses?"

A "Actually they're anti-flashbulb glasses. I have cameras going off in my face all day long. I don't mind the attention but now and then my eyes need a break. I manufacture them by the way and you can purchase a pair at For Eyes on the 4th floor or on my website."

"Santa has a website?" Kacy whispered to Jody. He dutifully looked it up on his phone and there it was. All sorts of Santa items were for sale. Hats, beards, eyebrow whitener, boots and gloves etc. Finally Santa Suits $500 (Dry clean only). There was also an online application for his world renowned Santa School.

Q "How many hours a week do you spend in your workshop making toys?"

A. "Contrary to what you may have heard, now-a-days I don't have time to make most of the toys. The elves do. I'm just the delivery man."

Q "Are you a method actor, do you ever seem trapped in your character?"

A "I am the real Santa and you can ask me what I'm feeling."

Q "And what are you feeling?"

A "Merriment!"

This Santa was media savvy and like many politicians he knew the names of most reporters even requesting his favorites be in attendance knowing the personal touch would make them write more favorably of him.

Q "Off the record how does it feel to be the highest paid Santa in the world?"

A "It's a dubious distinction since most of my Santa assistants work pro bono or just enough to cover expenses. Besides I donate all my profits to many charities around the world."

Q. "Can you name a few?"

A "The Salvation Army, I like their outfits and their willingness to stand out in the cold to help others, the Red Cross, many other charities and food banks, and also to Greenpeace. For full transparency the list is posted on my site."

Q. "With climate change is it true that the polar caps are melting?"

A "I'm afraid so. I'm in the process of moving my entire operation to the South Pole."

Q " Hi, I'm Marion from the Clarion. I just finished your autobiography 'Santa the Lean years' You were very slim in the cover photo."

A "So I was in those days, but Mrs. Claus is fond of saying that persistence overcomes. It does and with success I've fattened up over the years."

Q "How do you justify being so overweight with that being such a health problem these days?" asked a reporter from Channel 5 news.

A "Actually I'm not that chubby." replied Santa a little irritated now. "Much of what you see is padding keeping in line with the traditional Santa look. All my Santa assistants have padding in their suits."

Q "How many letters do you get every year?"

A "Very few children write letters anymore. Most of them just text me."

Even the parents admitted that this was the coolest Santa they had ever seen and many lined up for photos with him later that were taken by a very tall black bear with a very large camera. It was fun to think that Santa was real. When you really think about it, if you could get adults to reconsider the existence of Santa or even just the concept the world could be a better place.

Q. "Do you have a favorite Christmas song?"

A. "I saw mommy kissing Santa Claus." he chuckled.

"We have time for one last question."

Q "Where do you vacation?"

A "We have a working ranch in Montana."

Q "What are you raising there?"

A." What station are you from?"

A "Channel 5 news."

A "I don't know who you Channel 5 reporters are. I asked for the Giraffe guy, what happened to him?"

# VI

*Santa's Palace* was located on a street affectionally entitled 34th Street next to *The Tree* which had to be the eighth wonder of the World. It towered over the village like a benevolent volcano. Macintosh had shelled out A LOT, making it the world's most expensive Christmas tree. It looked like your average one hundred and fifty foot Norway Spruce but it boasted four hundred thousand lights with every needle a point of light changing in color and intensity, sometimes just glowing or twinkling, sometimes forming words promoting specific stores or just well wishes for the season, a masterpiece of fiber-optic technology. Like a kaleidoscope or the Einstein Tile the same design was never repeated and with a push of a button you could change the tree's appearance adding digital tinsel, pinecones, ornaments or strings of lights. With another button you could envelop the tree and the

Santa village below with a light snow. It came with the guarantee of new software every year and was created by two young nerds from Silicon valley. This tree was manually controlled by an onsite keyboard or from the mall's centralized computer.

The central bank of servers which controlled everything in the mall was overseen by Mimi a programmer extraordinaire. She rarely left her domain nicknamed the cave, but enjoyed spending all day and into the night with her equally gifted assistants, tweaking various functions and soaking up the electromagnetic fields created by all the electricity surging through the cavern that was her workspace. To access this special section, the heart of the mall, there was a two factor security protocol. First you had to sing or hum the first 4 bars of the song of the day, followed by a retina scan. You had to be careful not to stay out too late at night as you might end up being scolded by this machine, with the severity determined by how red your eyes were. Like many who are highly talented Mimi was a bit eccentric, but like most of us she always named her computers, a personal attribute in an impersonal age. When asked once why she had two laptops plugged into the mainframe instead of just one, her response was " This one I call Rhett and this one is Ashley, and I just can't make up my mind which one I love more."

*The Tree* was an advertising bonanza getting more

press coverage than a Hollywood scandal. This was somewhat of an irritation to our Santa as he felt he should be the star at this time of year not being upstaged by a tree no matter how fantastical it was. Chrissy entered the Santa's Manor House where Santa was taking a break while his substitutes continued to entertain the children. He couldn't just walk off and leave an empty chair with a hundred people standing in line. Most children couldn't tell one Santa from another anyway due to the standardized costume and some Santas were actually women but the only way a child could tell that was if they pulled her beard. Many parents could tell the difference though and were slightly miffed having to deal with an imposter. They wanted the real Santa from the interview, the one that had been on television all week. Chrissy asked "Hello, how was your interview?" "Ok. Well received" he answered "but during Christmas in July could we locate Santa's Palace elsewhere in the Mall. I find this giant tree to be a distraction." A few minutes ago while in the public eye he was jolly as an elf and now he was getting a bit grumpy as he pled his case. Chrissy thinking fast to soothe his feelings and thinking to herself are all artists this temperamental? replied "But you are the star! Think of it this way, some people come to see *The Tree* because of all the hype and advertising and are pleasantly surprised to find the world's greatest Santa right next door!!" As this seemed to be working she changed the subject. "How is your wife?" Brightening he replied "She's at home baking brownies for this evening." "I meant your professional wife, is she around here somewhere?" "Oh she's over there doing a good business promoting fruitcake. Before becoming my famous Mrs. she had been a demonstrator in grocery stores, one of the best so I recruited her."

Chrissy wandered over to listen to Mrs. Claus and watch the demonstration in progress. "Fruitcake is the most misunderstood dessert in the world next to blood pudding. What most people don't understand is that fruitcake should be heated before serving." She took a sheet of hot slices out of a portable oven. "Heating softens it and brings out the juices. The main juices are molasses, bourbon, brandy and rum. A light film of butter or whipped cream will make a convert out of anyone." She handed out the finished samples to the eager waiting crowd. (Given the ingredients though some might wonder if it is legal to provide fruitcake to minors.) Generally fruitcake reminded most people of bricks, solid and tasteless, and bricks are sold on pallets. So far today Santa's good wife had sold four pallets of fruitcakes the equivalent of 800 bricks, not bad!

Chrissy climbed back into her little car and drove away admiring the Santa's elves' costumes as some of them waved to her. Their outfits were covered with bells so that they didn't whistle while they worked, they jingled. There were extra elves she noted, but at this time of year they were probably necessary because of the increasing crowds. Also the green lighting was particularly Christmassy. "I must congratulate Soozie on her attention to detail."

Off to one side *The Leaping Lizards*, an acrobatic troupe still in costume as frogs, were taking a break and drinking fortified water. Even frogs have to replace their electrolytes. One six foot bullfrog was busily getting the phone number of the cheese and salami sample girl at her kiosk. The next kiosk over was occupied by a slicer-dicer company. To demonstrate the product's effectiveness the proprietor chopped over five hundred onions per day, all the while keeping up an endless sales pitch. "No housewife can live without this little gadget. With it you can have a pizza with everything on it in a matter of minutes." The problem was that the kiosk was situated right in front of a perfume shop. The patron saint of perfumers is actually St Nicholas and rivers of perfume are sold at this time of year. He was also claimed as patron saint by sailors, fisherman, children, archers and an every expanding list due to his popularity. A verbal battle was in progress outside the shop. "We're trying to introduce a new line of perfume today and your onions are stinking up our entire store. On top of that you have the nerve to come in here and use our lotion samples any time you feel like it." "Working with onions chaps my hands." he explained matter-of-factly as if entitled.

A mall manager has to be part referee, psychiatrist, diplomat, coach and dictator. Fortunately all the mall's kiosks were on wheels. "Hook your kiosk up to my car and I'll tow you down the street." It was slow going but finally they stopped in front of *Josh's Deli,* owned by an former stand up comedian, and across from it was *Jimbo's Diner.* With all the foodstuffs now in proximity the odor problem was solved but inevitably they had their own set of complaints. Jimbo featured burgers, hot dogs and pretzels tasty enough to compete with any modern ball park. However, Josh was a purist. It could be the eighteen hundreds or present day but his sandwich recipes never changed. His deli counter sold meats by the pound and he often saved the best of the wurst for special high paying customers knowing they would happily pay for the authenticity. But he was the most proud of his own mustard that he created from a secret ages old family recipe. Chrissy entered Josh's and ordered a pickled herring. Josh complied and Chrissy rolled her eyes. "Can I have it on a plate please?" Josh had the same problem as many comedians, whenever he opened his mouth people weren't sure where the comedy ended and the reality began. "Free potato salad for everyone present, compliments of the mall manager here." "What's the joke?" asked Chrissy. "No joke." Then Josh explained

THE NIGHT VISITORS | 55

his issue with Jimbo. "It's my mustard. Jimbo serves small mustard packets with each of his orders but the packets are too small and the mustard very bland so his customers walk over here and steal my mustard all day long and that is a lot of mustard!" What would you suggest?" asked Parlett empathizing with his problem. "Move that mooch to another location and put in a nice yogurt shop over here, or I could administer him a swift knuckle burger!" "I have a better idea." offered Parlett. "If you arranged with Jimbo to sell him special batches of your mustard in bulk at a fair price his customers would stay over at his shop to enjoy his meals. They'd be happy and you would have been compensated" "Why didn't I think of that, Ms. Parlett you are wise beyond your real years." Josh was familiar with her without her old lady costume as she often ordered a Ruben sandwich for lunch. Many of the mall's staffers ate here enjoying his old timey impromptu comedy. "May I have a half a chicken please" "Which half do you want the front half, the back half. the top half or the bottom half?" "How about whatever half you have available." "You don't walk into a butcher and ask for half a cow. You ask for a side of beef." " May I have a side of chicken please!" "Which side?"

After paying for his customers' potato salads Chrissy moved on. She passed two guys in a deer suit staring at the 3D holographic mall directory. "Can I help you?"

"No ma'am, we've already been given our assignment."
Another Soozie Beals' extra, but how did she get Bob
and Phil to wear that costume all day long.

Parlett put the car in gear in forward narrowly missing two dogs carrying half eaten sandwiches in their
mouths. The little car only had three gears, forward, stop
and backward. She wondered where all these pooches
came from. People moving away from the area often
dropped their dogs at the mall certain that the dogs
would be dealt with by the proper authorities not realizing that the proper authorities were too busy running
the mall. As their jobs were so new and they were just
learning the ropes the dogs were the least of their problems. Other dogs had escaped from the dog shows that
Soozie hosted. Dogs from all over the world competed for
top dog honors but some brave ones had sought asylum
by leaping over the ropes and disappearing through the
crowds, a Russian Wolf hound and a Siberian Husky
to name a few. Dogs especially liked hanging out near
*For the Birds* the mall pet shop. They didn't give a dog's
equivalent of a hoot about the birds, the fish or the
snakes either but there was always some broken dog
biscuits lying around and the faint hope that a customer
would adopt them since unlike the puppies in the store
they could be had for free. Looking from the dogs point
of view, what was the alternative to living in the mall.
For many a life on the run in the heartless streets or

that fatal shot in the paw when their usefulness was deemed over? They were highly motivated to remain free meaning that the dog catcher would be busy at his job for many hours that evening.

When she reached the miniature railroad depot Chrissy could immediately tell that the train had broken down. This scaled down locomotive was named *The Pastry Express* with cars designed as cupcakes and cookies. The ferring could be changed season by season. Currently it was the face of a gingerbread man, for Valentines it would be changed to a lollipop heart and Easter a pink rabbit etc. It was designed to go anywhere in the mall to the most popular sites, customer's requests and engineers discretion, since there were no tracks to follow. One of the mall's fountains was on the train's general route. It looked like a waterfall but it was actually a hologram. The passengers thought they would get soaked as they passed under it, but to their surprise it was actually a downrush of air, instead of H2O it was just O.

Two maintenance men were peering into side panels they had removed from the engine and were scratching their heads as they attempted to put the train back to rights. "What else is going wrong!!" She had witnessed several other malfunctions today, some escalators had stopped half way to their next floor and a bank of street lights had flickered off and on until they went dark. "We haven't had a problem all month, Ms. Parlett, it was running fine until a short while ago, but I will locate the issue and get it fixed. I think it is the computer connection or the software" "You know a lot about trains do you?" "My uncle was a hobo." he replied. At that moment the train came back on line as if by magic. "Just a minor glitch apparently and we have fixed it." Chrissy was skeptical and countered with "It seems to have fixed itself somehow but please report it if you have any more trouble." A full complement of toddlers standing in line were getting unruly from waiting and when the train was repaired and ready to run again it was push and shove just like their adult counterparts on a commuter train as they piled aboard.

# VII

*Gatewood* loved golf. As easy as it might seem to a neophyte, lining up a thirty foot putt took a trained eye, total concentration, and a soldier's solid nerves and steady hand. Every green posed a unique set of problems, virtually engineered by the world's finest course designers. The slightest miscalculation when lining up a shot meant serious trouble for an unflinching pro. This was *Putter's Island* the mall's miniature golf course where Gatewood liked to spend his days honing his skills. He reasoned that it wasn't that different from real golf. Sometimes it comes down to just one stroke. One stroke can mean glory or shame. Especially when people are watching, just like now. Gatewood was on his hands and knees, nose to the ground, studying the layout. The objective here was to get the ball past a flashing laser beam, then past a set of oversized pinball flippers, up a ramp and through a revolving triple access tunnel. One entrance led to a hole in one, another leading to a possible birdie and the third leading to another series of strokes that could end up with Captain Putter being dunked in a nearby lagoon. It worked this way. If you putted through the wrong tunnel it rolled down the trough into a bucket attached to a waterwheel that revolved then dropped it into the mouth of a crocodile that found it indigestible and spit it into the air where a croc poacher with a cricket bat smacked it into a target connected to a rod that was holding up a plank which dropped at the ring of a bell and the scowling Captain Putter waving a cutlass dropped feet first into the water. "Arr shiver me timbers!! I'll rip ya limb from limb and feed you to the barracudas." That was his curse. Hit the right tunnel and automation took care of the details. The ball rolled out into a catapult which launched it into a cup where a cybernetic cockatoo picked it up and dropped it into the hole for a perfect score.

In other words this was crucial business because the payoff for a hole in one was phenomenal from his point if view. The player won a free round of golf, a Jolly Roger soda glass, a surprise package from the Captain's treasure chest for himself and his entire party, plus a pair of tickets to Captain Putter's Invitational Summer classic. Gatewood took a few practice strokes. He wasn't worried about hitting the correct tunnel because he had sneaked in early in the morning and marked it with a tiny scratch. His perfect putt was on the road to glory, a thing of beauty, like a shooting star on a summer night, until three inches in front of the ramp, where it stopped dead, right under the sole of a polkadot sneaker. Gatewood stifled a holler, actually biting the grip on his brand new putter which he carried around in a case like a cue stick.

"Isn't it a little early in the day for you to be playing Miniature Golf?" "Elsie it took me ten minutes to line up that shot." "Don't you think ten minutes is a long time to play one hole?" "Not when you're trying to concentrate!" "I wasn't talking to you, I was talking to those people." There were three parties already lining up at the green waiting for him to finish and move on. They all nodded, then they gasped as he gestured as if to wrap his club around her skull. "One of these days..." "Oh Alexander you're so cute when you blow your stack." "Do me two favors Elsie, stay out of my life, at least for the rest of the day and stop calling me Alexander, I hate that name." "You're making a spectacle of yourself young man. You had better come over here and cool off. You are the assistant mall manager, act like it." Elsie picked up his golf ball, buffed it like a fallen plum then dropped it into her shopping bag.

Gatewood followed her across a footbridge to a rest area where her little wagon was parked next to a bench,

"Why do you lug that thing around all day?" "These bags get heavy." She reached into one of those bags removed a Venus De Milo candle and took out a lidded container. "I brought you a nice hot bowl of tomato soup." "I don't like tomato soup." "It's good for you, better than those hot dogs you are always eating. Do you know what they put in those things?" 'I don't care if they put real dog in them. You're not my mother." "No, just your grandmother. Someone has to keep an eye on you." "Give me back my golf ball!" "First drink the soup!" "Don't be ridiculous. Now I have to play that hole all over again." "Don't you have anything better to do?" "What's better than playing golf!" Elsie rolled her eyes "This is miniature golf!"

Just then a bell rang and Captain Putter fell into the lagoon. "I've never been to a real golf course, is clown dunking part of the game? I'll bet his timbers is shivering now matey." Elsie peered over Gatewood's shoulder at poor Captain Putter fishing for his hat. "Did you know you have mustard on your tie? And weren't you wearing this same suit yesterday? This is the world's largest shopping venue with suits available off the rack or you could visit the *Custom Tailors and Haberdashery*. You should at least button your jacket if you want to look the part of a manager I'm trying to help you Alexander." "Why don't you help Parlett if you want to help somebody?" "She doesn't need my help, she needs your help."

"She doesn't want my help." "How do you know that?" "Because if I was in her position I wouldn't want my help either! Elsie you are becoming a public nuisance." "But everybody likes me." "Almost everybody." "Ms. Parlett likes me." "I wouldn't hide under her skirts if I were you." "Are you trying to get rid of her?" "That's none of your business." "Maybe you are trying to get rid of me?" "You need to face reality. You'd be much happier in a retirement facility. You'd have a roof over your head, three square meals a day, constant supervision. You'd make new friends." "I don't need supervision, and I have plenty of friends right here. At my age I see life as more of a fairytale and that's how it should be." She took a Tweety Bird pocketwatch out of her bag. "In fact I'm meeting some friends for lunch in a few minutes. Then later we're going to a puppet show. Do you like puppets?" "Can I have my ball back?" "What ball?"

ELSIE HAD A SECRET that no one except Gatewood, Flora and Sarge, the head of the security division knew. She actually lived at the mall. Macintosh knew that her independent personality would not fare well in a senior home and had created a penthouse apartment for her with a private elevator that would whisk her to any floor she wished. He reasoned that everything she needed was available to her here. Restaurants, medical attention, clothing stores, entertainment and most importantly she was friendly with most of the employees and shop keepers. Most of them guessed that she was a bag lady that just spent her daytime here much like the many mall walkers out getting their daily exercise. Mall walkers were a fixture in most malls but here they had formed a club. Whether they were training for some event or just out seeking mates they were good for business. They purchased all their outfits and equipment here and after a brisk walk there was nothing like a hearty breakfast at one of the many restaurants. Soozie Beals loved the mall walkers because it allowed her to host marathons within the mall on all twenty floors.

However, if the shopkeepers had been more observant they would have noticed that for a bag lady Elsie's 'rags' were quite upscale and not at all in character. Some assumed that she worked part-time as she was often observed watering plants while seemingly talking to herself. She was seen picking up the odd pieces of trash and she always had money to pay her way, unlike Mr. Gatewood who expected everyone to comp him on their goods and services. Ironically he would always leave a tip but generally that never approximated the actual cost of the goods. Servers in the food courts especially dreaded his approach as he had often taken the entire plate of samples instead of one piece on a toothpick. "What are you doing?" "These are free samples aren't they?" "Yes," "So what's the problem!"

As Elsie moved off Gatewood reconsidered her admonishments but of course given his personality they were the wrong ones. Maybe it was time he exerted more control. He had managed to slip a couple of eviction notices in the rent letters he had left for Parlett to distribute. Those inhabitants of Wimpole Place were just taking up space, especially those Clovers, and that Obujati fellow. His uncle Macintosh didn't seem to care if they made money or not but Gatewood wanted only shops that turned a big profit quickly. He already had a wine merchant interested in their adjacent locations, so much more profitable than candles and exotic dust. By next week he'd send in the movers and the cleanup crew and by the end of the week the merchants of Wimpole place would have a Sommelier for a new neighbor and they will drink a toast to his success. (His success not the wine merchants.) He could handle Parlett because once it's done she couldn't undo it which would make her appear to be an indecisive leader. He didn't care much for the puppet show either. The puppeteer seemed to work only when he felt like it which was when he appeared to be sober, which wasn't often.

Gatewood wanted the perfect balance sheet for year end that he could take credit for and so to lessen employee costs he had given the maintenance team and most of Sarge's security team the evening off. Not to mention that in his estimation there were far too many elves at

Santa's Palace and he had told them to knock off early also. Besides they were a surly bunch with their Santa's Elves Union always making demands.

THE OTHER PARTICIPANT IN Elsie's secret was Sarge and he ran a tight security ship. His first name was Singer but everyone called him Sarge. He was a retired drill instructor and carried over this philosophy to Mall protection. The Public Is No Bargain. He was one of the very first employees of the mall and had been assigned at the ground breaking to guard the Champagne. His staff consisted of forty security guards, so two per floor. The official motto of the team was Nothing Gets Past Us. Like the English policemen of old they did not carry guns because that would usually create more problems than solve them and no one wants to shop in an armed camp. They usually wore blazers with the raspberry crest on the pocket, so they would appear to be like docents in a museum but they did wear bulletproof vests under their shirts and carried stunners since you never knew what the other guy would do. Today some were wearing costumes apropos to whichever floor they were assigned to.

Their duties ranged from watching for shoplifters to observing any shoppers faking slips and falls. Those fakers should have known better because the mall was equipped with cameras everywhere. Cameras in the trees, the fountains and many of the mannequins. Some of the strategically placed cameras had two way audio occasionally commanding a would be shoplifter to Put that back on the shelf. You are being recorded. Those cameras also doubled as check in stations much like the call boxes employed by London Bobbies in the 1800's to call into Scotland yard. "Mommy, why is that officer talking to that tree". They were called Bobbies after their creator an Englishman named Robert Peel. In addition to the officers it was rumored among the mall staff that some of the teenagers who roamed the mall with their friends were actually functioning as under-cover agents to report any suspicious goings on like Sherlock Holmes' irregulars. Sarge had theorized that if they were given an actual purpose for being there, they would then stay out of trouble themselves. Also he gave them classes on basic security so they could help without causing a disruption.

All the cameras looped into a huge bank of TV moni-tors inside the security office and recordings were made. A great example that Sarge liked to recall was when he had spied the same guy walking through the mall in a suit day after day. Examining the records he had become suspicious. After a few days it turned out that the man was a thief. He was stealing suits.

The information gleaned from the recordings didn't stop with security. They also provided excellent marketing data. How long patrons stayed in a store, how long they stared at a window display, male vs female behavior patterns. Women like to try on clothes, a man might try on a jacket. Women love to try on shoes and model them in the mirror, most men rarely even open the box. A larger percentage of women did the serious shopping which was a contradiction from olden days. In ancient Athens women were not allowed in the marketplace, or even allowed to leave their houses unless accompanied by the master, or another alpha male in the household. Now men typically just want to get it over with so they could leave, and will hurriedly grab a few items suitable or not, and since women have no problem returning things, most men just have their wives do it if necessary. The guards were also expected to be babysitters since many parents would drop their kids off at the mall and not pick them up until hours later and with all the cameras it made it easy to keep tabs on them. So not only is big brother watching you, but big momma, big grandpa, and big aunt.

# VIII

*Rental letters* in hand, Chrissy drove on now intent on getting them all delivered. There was the tobacco shop *Raliegh's Recommendations*. Every variety and flavor of tobacco was represented so that a mixture of cherry bon-bon, apricot wine, peaches and crème and coco among others combined to blanket this part of the street with overpowering scents to lure passersby into the store. The tobacconist was smoking in his doorway again and staring through the window of the nearby dance studio *En Pointe* pining away like a lovesick poet. 'All is dross that is not Helene'. The ballet teacher was dancing alone which she did every day at this time, floating to her own private aria like the last lily in the pond. Her name was Helen but she added the extra E after consulting her numerologist. (on the second floor.) In addition to his vast selection of cigars and snuff the tobacconist sold imported cigarettes piecemeal and the high point of his day was when she locked her studio and came across the street and into his shop for her daily Galois.

The clock maker *Such Watch* further on was working on one of his inventions called a Bolshoi Clock. On the hour, instead of a trap door, a tiny curtain goes up and the dancer lifts the ballerina over his head, spins her around, glides her down and they go back in and the curtain falls, then Russian kick dancers would appear on the half hour. His store featured every clock imaginable. There were large but scaled down replicas of Big Ben and even countertop versions although he hadn't quite figured out how to replicate that deep bong in miniature so they counted off the hours at a slightly higher pitch. There were alarm clocks, wrist watches, stop watches and even a few clock radios, not old enough to be antiques but still representative of another age. There were classic pocket watches made of gold and silver but also pocket watches and wrist watches as well with interchangeable cartoon faces depending on your daily comedy level. A highly rare Quail clock was on display which uttered woook, woook instead of cuckoo, cuckoo on each hour, a nice change of pace.

The value of time changes with the times. Once there was only daytime and nighttime. Then there were calendars, lunar calendars, then leap years. But how far did a leap year leap? (It took centuries to figure it only leaped one day over all that time.) There were sundials, hour glasses and candle clocks. In one corner was a replica of King Alfred's candle clock. (The original would have been 1100 years old at this point so it had to be a replica.) Then came real clocks. Now there was wasted time, personal time, down time, precious time, time zones, time tables, time clocks. Then came atomic clocks, fractions of seconds adding up to hours, nanoseconds adding up to days, milliseconds to years, microseconds to centuries, picoseconds to millenniums, femtoseconds to infinities, and only a computer could tell how many zeros were in a femtosecond. Time equals distance divided by speed, but how far and how fast? Is time circular or is it curved, warped, bent and twisted like space? Time is a dimension but which dimension? Fourth, fifth, sixth? And how many damn dimensions are there? Thought experiments produce as many questions as answers. How fast do thoughts travel? How long does it take to come to a single conclusion, and how conclusive are conclusions? Time is not absolute or is it? Is time made up of particles like protons? Ticks become Tocks. Circadian clocks spin both ways. Will these questions ever be answered? Maybe time will tell.

Macintosh had lent the clockmaker a small Dali painting of Soft Clocks which he had proudly hung on the wall above a cabinet displaying a selection of molded Soft Clocks in various sizes that you could hang over a shelf or wine rack. The store even had a digital doomsday clock rapidly counting down to the time when humans will have obliterated themselves through wars or simply lack of care for our precious planet. The red numbers indicated that we still had time left if we used it wisely. Would we?

Next door there was an antique shop, which made her wonder what antique shops sold in the old days when everything was new. (And maybe still was.) Rare, Antique, Authentic, three signposts that often led to intrigue. Collectors of anything fell under their spell, searching for the masterpiece in the miser's attic, the lost work in the used bookstore, the misminted coin or stamp. The signs pointed to mansions, museums, galleries, up the palace steps or down dark alleyways looking for the ultimate prize. Each antique or collectible this shop sold came with certificates of authenticity, signed by experts, and included their phone numbers and addresses in case customers wanted to do some fact-checking which was strongly advised in the disclaimer.

Christmas wouldn't be Christmas without a choir and there were several choirs of various sizes situated throughout the mall. She passed a pink cheeked cheery group untiringly running through their repertoire of classical, religious and secular tunes. They were accompanied by a string trio comprised of a violin, a cello and a harpist all three perched on a revolving plinth. Music is more sparkly when played on a harp, sounding more authentic like a music box of old adding to the nostalgia that everyone feels at this time of year. Carolers strolled by. They were called The Eves. They were dressed like Puritans, two Goodys and three Preachers. She found this strange because in days past hadn't the Puritans outlawed Christmas?

Parlett stopped to check her schedule then drove away passing a survey taker, another of Soozie's ideas to use for future marketing. However sometimes novice survey takers ask the wrong questions to the wrong passersby.

Q "How many pets do you own?"

A. "Counting fish, about five thousand." It was Bella the pet store owner opening up for the day. She was cradling a gray and white skunk in her arms.

Q "That's strange color for a skunk?"

A "He's getting old and going gray." She scratched the back of his neck and he began to purr.

Q "What did you get for Christmas last year?"

A "A reprieve from the governor." Answered a swarthy looking gentleman.

Q. "How far do you live from here?"

A "Approximately fourteen thousand kilometers Comrade." smiled a petite lady wearing a huge fur hat.

Q " How often do you and your wife dine out?"

A " Three times a day"

Q. "Three times a day?"

A " We're Truckdrivers!"

He finally saw a shopper in a nice business suit looking dapper except for the dapple of mustard on his tie.

Q. "Excuse me sir. Do you work in this mall?"

A "Yes"

Q. "What was the last beverage you drank?"

A. "Five or six samples of eggnog from that robot over there."

Q "Do you like your job?"

A "Do you???"

CHRISSY PASSED STREET MUSICIANS, who were actually professional musicians paid to look like street musicians. Now and then a real street musician intent on busking, would sneak in, throw down his hat and play until the hat was full. Better music, fuller hat. There was a snake charmer with what appeared to be a tone deaf cobra and a man dressed as an eight foot candy cane. Loose flying balloons moved to-and-fro as the balloon seller tried unsuccessfully to recapture them, impossible once they were loose. It was the day before Christmas and every creature imaginable was astir including a character on a fifteen foot unicycle (a Penny Farthing) who called himself Tinsel Man as he peddled by covered in loose foil and tinsel from his head to his bicycle pedals. Over his arm he carried a basket full of lightbulbs. Because of his height he cycled around replacing burned out bulbs as needed in the one story high streetlamps.

There were numerous coffee shops in the mall and like so many shoppers needing a boost, Chrissy stopped at the Starving Artists Café and navigated past the tables of would be writers, and poets for a quick Espresso and a Beignet wondering if these were real artists creating their masterpieces as many artists had done in many cafes in the past or another Soozie Beals extra to create ambiance for the tourists as they certainly didn't appear to be starving.

She soon encountered another traffic jam in her travels. The streets were bumper to elbow like downtown Delhi. Crowds of shoppers had gathered to watch a high wire act featuring Slippy the Clown. Slippy had graduated from clown college (anyone interested www.

clowncollege.com) and incorporated being a clown into his high wire act. He felt that it would be less scary and more fun for the kiddies to watch if a clown walked the wire. He never did anything stupid like walking a wire over the Grand Canyon or Niagara Falls. He was strictly a second story man as most malls had just two floors. This mall had twenty floors but Slippy wasn't crazy enough to walk a wire over twenty floors so he continued on with two. Besides, he liked to work without a net, it just looked more real, and with just two floors he could set up a host of props to fall into. Most of the time it was deliberate. He would appear as a man in a business suit complete with fedora and briefcase, start walking down the wire, slip on a banana peel, start wobbling and fall off into a giant banana crème pie below.

The next time he appeared he was in his clown costume and walked the wire using balloons instead of a balancing pole. The balloons were filled with helium and confetti. Navigating the wire was no easy feat in his twenty five inch clown shoes size forty and inevitably he slipped and slided, several times for maximum effect, and as he fell into a giant bowl of jello below the balloons popped and the crowd below was covered in red and green confetti. The crowd loved this but understandably he wasn't a favorite of the clean up crew.

His third act involved the high wire being transformed into an electrical wire with a giant transformer at one end. (In the clown world everything had to be oversized to be it's funniest.) As he danced across the wire his giant feet sizzled, burst into flames and emitted smoke as the wire appeared to light up like lightening bolts. When he made it to the other side the crowd cheered. Slippy bowed then fell into a giant goldfish bowl, his flaming feet extinguished and the crowd moved on. Shortly after a flock of birds returned and took up their positions back on the wire which they thought was their own personal landing space.

*The Magic Hat* was a combination magic show and trick shop. Costumes for any occasion were for rent or sale, not just for Halloween but parties, weddings and any event whose slogan was Don't Come As You Are. This is also where Soozie obtained costumes for all the mall's employees. Twice a day the shop hosted magic shows featuring TaDa The Magician and his assistant Presta. They were an odd couple always arguing during the performances. "I will now make my assistant disappear." She stepped into a cupboard. He waved some scarves then reopened it. She was still there, arms folded tapping her foot. "What happened? You're still here?" "I'll disappear when I feel like it!" " Well now it's time to get into this box so I can saw you in half." "You're not paying me enough to do that, I want a raise." "We can talk about that later after the performance." "No talk, I want it now, in advance!" and she stormed off the stage. Undeterred TaDa proceeded to work the crowd, pulling chocolate coins out from behind customers ears and a rabbit out of his top hat. Not to be outdone Presta pulled wads of cash out of the hat. Parlett approached them. "Can you pull a rent check out of the hat?" TaDa pulled the check from behind Parlett's ear. "Hey wait a minute this check is blank." "Don't worry the invisible ink only takes fifteen minutes to appear." "It had better or I'll make your store disappear!" Just then the lights in the shop flickered out. The patrons thought this was part of the show and cheered but Chrissy knew better. Everything had been running so smoothly for months and now on this important day the malfunctions were stacking up. System overload or something else, so she made a note and drove on hoping to find the answer.

## IX

*L*ittle Kacy had wanted to visit Santa now that the Santa interview was over and make her Christmas wishes perfectly clear but the line was very long and as she and Jody walked away the gatekeeper handed them little booklets titled How To Be Nice For The Following Year. "We already do all this things!" said Kacy disappointed that she wasn't going to visit with Santa but thinking of this pamphlet as a validation. She was confident now that all her wishes would be filled. They wandered over to the video arcade and spent an hour or so playing video games while keeping a watchful eye on the Santa line but the line only got longer. Jody won some games this time although his sister remained champion as usual much to his irritation.

Getting low on change they left and then spied what appeared to be an authentic royal red Gypsy wagon with a small queue of customers waiting to get in. The sign said Madame Angelica Futurologist. Some in the mall wondered what a gypsy fortune teller had to do with Christmas. The answer was: Nothing. But she was doing record business making predictions for the upcoming new year. This was another of Soozie's better ideas. She had found this gypsy on the internet and as it was the new millennium, gypsys with websites could be expected. Something had seemed to move her hand to select this one from the list, or perhaps it was just that she was fascinated by the wagon.

When it was their turn Kacy and Jody entered. The inside of the wagon appeared to be much, much larger than the outside of the wagon which was strange. A voice said "Are you children here to have your fortunes told?" "Not me. Just her." Said Jody as always skeptical of anything supposedly otherworldly. Madame pointed to a plush purple couch, a two seater, as most people were reluctant to venture in there alone. Kacy asked what was most on her mind. "Where do you keep the horse for the wagon?" Madame answered. "You'll notice this wagon requires two horses. They stay in a horse hotel." Kacy knew this was all the answer she was going to get. Madame continued "how would you like me to proceed? There are several ways to look into the future. I could read your palm, I could use Tarot cards, or I could use the crystal ball." "O, use the crystal ball" said Kacy. "is it real crystal?" "I don't know what it is. It fell from the sky years ago, just as a comet was passing overhead." Madame rubbed the crystal ball closed her eyes and the crystal clouded up. Jody dropped a quarter on the floor so as to disguise his sneaking a peek under the table cloth. Madame was wearing red cowboy boots. (actually they were Cossack boots a family heirloom.) She appeared to have a foot operated control panel under the table which Jody guessed operated all the special effects in the crystal, the dimming and undimming of the lights, and the smoking candles off to the side next to jars marked exotic dust and other impulse purchases of incense burners, Ouija boards and miniature crystal balls (from smaller comets?) Prediction: "I see a great adventure ahead for you both with chaos and confusion. *You will meet a stranger. A cute little fellow. He will show you the way.*" She opened her eyes as the crystal clouded further with a faint green glow. Genuinely surprised she frantically rubbed the crystal ball which only made it greener, and in a low whisper to herself murmured "I didn't know they were here, I thought they were just stories that my grandmother told." Then recomposing herself she abruptly gestured for them to leave "Thank you Madame has another customer now!"

"Well that was fun." Like his dad Jody could be a bit sarcastic but this comment went over Kacy's head as she obviously took the prediction seriously. "We had better go to *The Treehouse* now to meet Grandma" she said as they exited the wagon which from the outside appeared to have resumed it's original size.

*The Treehouse* had a ground floor where roots were designed as tables which is where they were sitting but also for the right price you and your party could spend some quiet time out on your own limb higher up where you would be waited on by waiters and waitresses dressed in stylish leaves. Kacy and Jody finished their milkshakes which was all they could afford with their left over video arcade money and still no Grandma.

"You'd better call mom." said Kacy. Jody responded " She's very busy today and I don't want her to worry. Let's leave a message with the doorman. We'll swing by here later and meanwhile take a tour of the mall."

"Did I hear you say you wanted a tour?" They turned to see a boy about Jody's age dressed in what appeared to be a slightly shabby Victorian guttersnipe costume. Like the security guards all the tour guides were wearing costumes today. "Jack Dawkins is the name and I know every nook and cranny in this mall." "And how do you know that?" asked Jody. "I live here." Sure you do, thought Jody but being adventurous he said "Sure, lead the way" "We'll start with pastry and lunch places," replied Jack. "You look like you might still be hungry. All the shop keepers give me free samples to test out."

The nearest elevators were constructed of tubular

clear glass, rotating as they ascended or descended, and instead of going straight up and down they wound like Archimedian Screws. They headed for the tenth floor.

*The Rue de Cordon* was the main boulevard in *The French Quarter* a minicourt. There were clotheslines hanging out of the windows of dress shops dangling with the latest fashions. The mannequins in the shop windows had no heads or hands because the manufacturers had calculated they could save twenty five percent on the cost of wood or plastic. There were steaming sewers for authenticity. (But thankfully no authentic sewer tours). The streetlights were programmed to come on at seven to give a taste of Parisian nightlife. A lone French Poodle, without a collar, sat staring at a sidewalk artist who would masterfully sketch or paint your portrait and there was a Gendarme strolling back and forth. Today the Gendarme was actually Sarge in costume. His security crew rotated sections on a revolving schedule so they wouldn't become typecast. Every minicourt in the mall had appropriately dressed constables, Bobbies for *London Town*, town Marshalls for *Old Tombstone*, Ninjas for old and new Tokyo etc. Sarge didn't eat full meals on duty, just snacks since he would daily walk off the calories. This was his favorite floor and when not here he frequented *The Cupcakery* (on the 5th floor) shaped like a twenty foot cupcake. With your order they featured bite sized cupcakes, free but you were expected to leave a tip. If you didn't the cupcake turned red and menacing and a voice came over the loudspeaker and hollered cheapskate. After that, understandably, the tips rolled in.

The kids walked into Emile's pastry shop followed by Sarge. It had exposed brick walls and columns and wood plank floors. There was a section where College students worked on their projects sipping espresso or sampling wine, and being French Emile provided a private dining section for lovers. There were antique bakery cabinets with cakes on display as if they were 'objets d'art'. Featured on the menu board were pastries from all over the world baked-to-order while you wait. Cannolis from Italy, Strudel from Austria, Kringle from Denmark, and cupcakes from America. There were state-of-the-art ovens that looked old and authentic, and naturally they cost twice as much as ovens that looked new. Emile graciously divulged his recipes to anyone who asked but they were so complex and contained so many hard to find ingredients that it was cheaper and easier to just buy the finished pastries from him.

"Bonjoir Jacques." Apparently the shopkeepers did know Jack. "Who are your friends?" "This is Kacy and Jody. What recipes are you testing today?" "I call it Bomb Bread, a recipe I pinched from the Italians. They call it Bomba. It is a loaf of bread which bakes up hollow inside full of hot air like a larger version of a Popover.

Touch it with a knife and....Boom." "It explodes?" asked
Sarge. Emile replied "A very tiny explosion." Sarge
touched it with a knife and there was a very big explosion. Crumbs flew everywhere. "Hmmm I think it needs
a little something. An entire batch ruined." Sarge countered with "I think it has a little too much something."
Emile explained "This is why I give out free samples
only to my favorite regulars. What if this happened to
a paying customer!" The Café's waiter brought the little
trio their turnovers and Jack said "just a minute!" as he
pricked the turnovers with a knife, .. just in case.

"So Sarge, what's the latest, have there been any
break-ins?" Sarge chuckled "This mall is burglar proof.
Too many employees here day and night. We are staffed
in full during the day and on the night crew we have
ten janitors, five maintenance men, and a twenty man
security team. Every staff member has an electronic
identification tag and without it you would get locked
up immediately." "Where do you put people without a
tag?" "Beats me I never caught anyone without a tag."
"What about shoplifters?" "Different story. It amazes
me what people risk their freedom for: bobby pins, key
chains, Christmas cards. Why last week I caught an
elderly gentleman lifting a beak sharpener from the pet
store for his Parakeet. I felt sorry for him and let him go.
The very next day I caught him stealing a Parakeet for
his Parakeet. He had it right there in his breast pocket

upside down so the feathers sticking out looked like a handkerchief, but I noticed that the color of the handkerchief didn't match his outfit. A revealing no, no."

"Very clever of you Sarge. Well perhaps you could look into this for me? I am missing some vital shipments today that I will need for Monday, some special extra fine flour and imported butter that should have been delivered hours ago." Sarge nodded and made a note on his clip board. Then Emile handed him a small jar marked exotic dust. " Merry Christmas Sarge. No charge. It will bring you luck." Emile and Sarge were chatting away when Henri, Emile's neighbor stormed into the shop. "Crumbs, crumbs, everywhere...." "Ah my arch enemy." Emile said to Sarge. "Please excuse me I must go quarrel with him." "...their sticky fingers all over my garments. They come in here, they eat and when this monster is done with them they are too fat to fit into my dresses. This man is destroying my business! I'm going to request to be relocated..." Being French, Henri is very passionate. "... and your sign *Rageneau's Pastry Shop*. You should be ashamed of yourself." Henri had a sign over his dress shop door also. It said *Bovary's*.

X

*Say Cheese* was Chrissy's next stop. It was actually a photo shop, picture frames, passport photos, telescopes and high end cameras and appeared to be a great success. The owner was an ex New Yorker who had previously sold cameras in the mishmash that was Times Square. "Cameras, cameras, highest quality, get them here." Surprisingly he was legit which is why he had opened a shop in the mall no longer able to compete with the so called bargain prices of the questionable merchandise hawked by the dubious competitors back home. He was also a friend of Josh and Jimbo, all three if them transplants from back east.

She then entered *Temporary Tatts*, a tattoo parlor for the indecisive. The tattooed store mannequins sported mohawks and pierced body parts. If you stared long enough they appeared to move slightly. (Which was because they were actually live models.) The artist would project your desired tattoo design onto your skin and then sprayed biodegradable ink over the stencil. Instant tattoo, but after two weeks of soap and water the tattoo would disappear and you could choose to have it redone or forget about it. Or you could just select from a variety of stick-ons, very popular, inexpensive and very temporary. In addition they sold high end clothing imported from London, properly ripped and torn, which for a fee you could wear for a week and then return for a new set (and a new fee). In short it cost a pretty penny to look impoverished.

BACK AT THE OFFICE Flora was going over the checklists preparing for Monday morning when all the celebrities and dignitaries would be in attendance for the Grand Opening festivities. Every business establishment has an opening and later an official opening after the kinks are worked out and they were certainly experiencing their share of kinks today. She had received numerous calls regarding various malfunctions such as doors becoming automatically locked or lights switching off. Even Sarge had called to request electricians as many of his security cameras and recorders were on the fritz.

Gatewood wandered in. "Flora can I have my messages please." "You don't have any messages, in fact you never have any messages." "Just the way I like it" he responded as he headed towards his office. Once out of sight he detoured to the left and entered Parlett's office. He liked to sit in her chair and imagine himself in command. He mentally composed the lists of employees that he would be firing, Flora would definitely be on it, and he practiced his speech that he hoped would humiliate them for all the supposed slights he had suffered. He had no way of knowing that Flora had been tasked by Macintosh to report on Gatewood's behavior good or bad directly to him on a regular basis.

Parlett's office was still in the completion stage, the exposed vents and beams giving it a comfortable bohemian feel, and to rectify this he had already placed an order for new furniture telling the purveyor that he would firm up the delivery date the following week. At last as the scion, he would be able to take his rightful place in the Macintosh corporation. He might even have the new wine merchant that would open up on Wimpole place send him over his most expensive bottle of wine (gratis of course) so he would be able to celebrate. Why Parlett wasted her time visiting stores was totally beyond his comprehension. Once he took over he planned to spend his days either here relaxing in the office or out at the golf course as any manager should.

PARLETT WAS MAKING PROGRESS. *The Grand,* the piano store for virtuosos and professionals, was hosting an impromptu performance by maestro pianist Remi Fasilado. His nimble fingers brought to life the music of Waltzes In Winter Smoke by Vengolt the gypsy composer. He imagined himself as a modern day Franz List and wore a period outfit to emphasize this. Actually he wore this outfit everyday not just on days when costumes were required and he was never seen without it, almost a musical Dracula. In fact it did sell pianos. Most of the store's clientele were symphony companies world wide but millionaires often liked to purchase a Grand Piano or a Baby Grand to display in their drawing rooms even though most of them rarely played. Good for parties though.

Next to one of the food courts was *The Raspberry Hill Book Fair.* This location was based on the theory that many people like to read while eating lunch and outside the bookstore was a magazine stand catering to those with only a short lunch break and no time to browse. The store itself was always filled with customers, unusual for a mall bookstore. This was due to the constant flow of authors and celebrities promoting and signing their books which ranged from fluff pieces, confessions and revelations to serious works. Cookbooks were especially popular primarily those written by chefs that owned restaurants, but also those written by public figures who usually knew nothing about cooking and employed the cooking equivalent of ghost writers. This store could locate any book ever printed and in whatever language and have it shipped to you or even print out a copy for you with the push of a button. Especially popular at this time of year for gifts were children's talking books (batteries included) which read aloud as the child turned each page relieving frazzled parents from that duty. Whether you were a bookworm or a magazineworm, a movieworm or a musicworm, classics old and new were available. Positioned near the exit were three small girls in woodlands costumes selling bunches of The World's best Mistletoe. In two months they would be selling Girl Scout cookies. Many highly successful future saleswomen had gotten their start this way.

Right next door was *Baby Boomers* featuring various nostalgia items such as Nehru jackets and hippy clothes, Edgar Allan Poe movie posters and coffee table books such as Elvis Explained and The British Invasion Explained. Complete your model collection with a miniature Robby the Robot (assembly required) or a life size Sputnik model. Rounding out that street was The Souvenir Shop full of mall keepsakes for the packrat in the family, keychains, mugs, T-shirts, placemats and the like.

By now most shoppers had no empty hands or shoulders and fortunately for them Raspberry Hill provided a valet service that wrapped your gifts and then took your packages to your car and loaded them for you freeing you up to begin again after a short break. All afternoon long these couriers could be seen carrying presents large and small to their destinations. Especially today this service was doing a booming business. There was no charge for this although many shoppers tipped the delivery people who happily pocketed the ten or twenty percent they were gifted. Shoppers could then relax in private rooms entitled *Rest Up Rooms* for a small fee where for 15 or 30 minutes they could lay down on couches in complete silence to rejuvenate, get their second wind and then attack their shopping lists with renewed vigor.

All malls have cellphone stores, appliance stores and electronics stores but here even these had something extra, something unique. The customer associates actually knew their products inside out, and helped their customers by steering them to the items that were best for the customer and not just for the bottom line. Chrissy stopped at each one. She examined the latest in hand held communication and recording devices, purchased a new battery and moved on as best she could through the crowds. There was a mime directing foot traffic, but people kept pushing him aside.

When she arrived at *The Uppercrust,* the mall's premiere cake and pie store, she could barely get through the door because racks and racks of cooling pies almost blocked her way. "What's this all about?" she asked the worried looking pastry chef who replied "I'm getting kind of nervous. If someone doesn't come by to pick up this pie order soon I'll be stuck with all 300 of them. You know that I advertise that all goods are baked fresh daily which means I cannot sell them two days from now on Monday." Who ordered them perhaps we can give them a call?" asked Chrissy. "The order was placed over the internet and I've tried calling but cannot get through." He explained. Privately she though this to be very suspicious and was beginning to suspect sabotage. Just one more unexplainable event that she added to her list vowing to herself that she would get to the bottom of whatever was going on. "Well don't worry" responded Chrissy. If they don't show up we can donate these pies to a homeless shelter to add to their Christmas dinner and you can write them off.

As befitting the season Macintosh had ordered in a beautiful Nativity scene. The figurines in the crèche were almost luminescent and had been hand carved by artists from the Holy Land. Parlett turned off her engine, sat silently and felt uplifted by the quiet space that the scene commanded. However she soon realized that something was missing, there were no wisemen. She hoped this was just a shipping mistake and not a sign of the times and since she had personally placed the order she ran down a mental checklist. Nativity scene consists of Mary, Joseph, Infant and manger (straw included) plus two shepherds, one sheep, one goat, one cow, one camel, one donkey and three wisemen with accessories. Apparently some kind of wiseman or woman had previously been there because at Mary's feet someone had left a copy of Dr. Spock's Baby and Childcare. Shocked at first she then considered that perhaps that it was a well meaning gift, no more outlandish than a song, a tin drum, a box of gold or oils and spices from the orient, and since no customers had complained yet she left it there hoping all would be forgiven as promised.

## XI

*J**ack Dawkins*** looked at his watch. "We had better get a move on as the Ice Show is about to start downstairs and you don't want to miss that especially if you love ice skating which includes just about everybody." As they headed to the elevators to go down to the show Jody noticed that the clothing shop mannequins now had heads with eyes that seemed to follow them as they walked along. There have always been folks who looked at a poster from any angle and felt the eyes were following them and in the case of these mannequins they probably were. "Are they part of the security features?" he asked Jack. "Probably, they keep changing things around, I just work here." replied Jack a little furtively. Jody wondered about the non committal answer. It was his prerogative, but was Jack keeping something important from them?

Kacy asked Jack. "Do your parents work here too?" "I don't know my parents." responded Jack "If you don't have parents how do you know your name?" asked the saddened Kacy. "Some of the salesladies gave me that name. They said I reminded them of someone" "Who gave you permission to live here?' asked Jody who was starting to believe Jack's original story as everything he had said so far had been true. "There is a nice lady named Elsie that lives here and most of the time I stay at her apartment. She arranged for me to take some courses, but only the easy ones, Business Marketing, Accounting, Retail Management. She's my fairy god-mother." Kacy was impressed and smiled. "You have a fairy godmother?" As they exited the elevator Jody slapped his own forehead and rolled his eyes.

Jack, Jody and Kacy followed the signs to the giant indoor skating rink which was just past the indoor ski slope. Ski lifts operated year round because a controlled 25 degree temperature assured good powder every day. There were two Swiss chalet style rest stops one serving coffee and hot alcoholic beverages and one was a hot chocolate bar catering to the younger ski bums. To the side a snowman building contest with over fifteen entries had a winner. "Congratulations go to The Abominable Snow-woman." Immediately an argument broke out, the losing contestants insisting that this was a SnowMAN contest and that it was easier to create a snowskirt that try to carve out pants, but the ruling stood.

Down in the ice rink there was a hockey game finish-ing up and all the skaters had pony tails sticking out of their helmets. Kacy was delighted to see that girls could play professional hockey also. As soon as the game was over the ice was treated to a touch up by a custom made Zamboni designed as a choo choo train and operated by a Santa's elf at the wheel.

The lights dimmed as they took their seats. The upcoming matinee show was for kids but ice shows always have the effect of turning adults into kids again and have them wide eyed and laughing at the simplest of gags. The show started with a series of comedy sketches performed by top ranking figure skaters. Ice skating bears, clowns and cartoon characters who have not been modified to fit the small screen, wowed the crowd with their expertise. They were treated to excerpts of famous plays. An ice skating alligator ripped the seat out of Captain Hook's pants. Bungee jumpers who dove down onto the ice skated doing a series of flips and double flips then leapt back up to the floors overhead followed by a chorus line of ice dancers. The finale of act one was a group of skating crayons leaving eponymous trails on the ice of red, green, and blue creating a kindergartner style painting of a typical family, house, mom, dad, kids, dog and cat. The technology was astounding and the catchphrase heard in the audience became a how do they do it.

After the ice was rezambonied for Act two the arena went dark. Then came the classic whistling that opened the theme from West Side Story. One by one the spotlights came on, here a Jet there a Jet. These young hoodlums were on skates which had been repurposed to look like dirty sneakers. It was a fantastic performance even though neither Jody or Kacy understood it's origin. Jack explained "This is a classic movie of all classic movies. Do you like movies? Why don't we go see a movie after this. The theater is nearby."

Act three was next. It was the highlight of the show and one that Soozie Beals took the most pride in having signed up. It was called The Ribbons. The lights went down, spotlights came on which illuminated four white boxes with people lying on top of them. They were dressed in red, gold, green and silver. They were lying flat, giving the impression that they were wrapping paper ribbons but they were actually contortionists. Another spotlight came on which illuminated a girl skater with a gigantic pair of scissors. The Stevie Wonder song Ribbon In The Sky started to play as she spun from giftbox to giftbox in a series of triple loops and spirals awash in ice flakes engulfing her like her own personal raindrops. The spotlight followed her as she opened the scissors and began skating in circles doing a cartwheel now and then and scraping the people lying on the boxes. They contorted into unimaginable shapes like real ribbons and turned into bows. It was if the contortionists had rubber bones. When she was done the boxes now looked like beautifully wrapped presents As she started to exit one of the bows started to uncurl and go limp. She skated back and rescraped first an arm then a leg until the bow was restored and then she concluded with a perfectly executed backward scratch spin. The crowd gave them a four minute standing ovation.

JACK HAD NO SHORTAGE of places to show these new friends of his. He especially liked them because they were the first children he knew that were his own age since he had left the orphanage. He didn't remember his father but he did remember his mother, a beautiful woman, a shining angel in his dreams. And of course his kindly older uncle who had regretfully placed him in the orphanage because as a merchant sailor he was in no position to care for his young nephew. His sea travels kept him away from land for six months to several years at a time although they did communicate via letters which always took a long time to arrive from many exotic ports around the world. The orphanage was all right but very regimented and boring to young Jack, his imagination sparked by the colorful descriptions of far away places his uncle conveyed. The next time his uncle was on shore he convinced him to write the matron a letter allowing Jack to visit and stay with him for a while. It was all in the language. What was his uncle's intention of a necessary short visit before he shipped out again Jack had craftfully twisted the meaning to be for a long stay and so it was that the staff saw him off on the bus which carried him to the coast and then after a few days Jack headed back, not to return to his dull life, but directly to Raspberry Hill where adventure awaited which is what it said on the several billboards he had seen around town.

It was there that he had met Elsie, assisting her one day when her cart had tipped over spilling that day's treasures. He gallantly collected her goods for her and over lunch and a soft drink, his reward, he had communicated his situation. She was a good listener and not being a big fan of institutions herself and being predisposed to taking in strays, she suggested that he bunk in with her knowing that if he stayed in the mall at her place he would be safe.

THE TRIO PASSED *EXCHANGE* which advertised that you could change your Euros for a Mark, a Yen, a Buck or a Pound. The shop catered to the many visitors from far away countries sometimes seen walking in with large cases on wheels of their own currency only to leave with a small wallet full of crisp ten's and twenties such were the exchange rates. For their convenience the shop also sold an impressive selection of wallets. Jody wanted to go in to find coins to add to his coin collection but they barely had enough cash left to spend let alone exchange for fun. He made a note to visit another time.

Next door was *Build A Drone*. All the basic components were ready for assembly. When you finished the assembly process you were invited to try out your drone on the test range the theory being that you already bought it so go ahead and break it and then you could rebuy. (This could qualify as questionable marketing and had been reviewed by Gatewood who took home a new drone on the house assuring the proprietors that for the time being no changes needed to be made.) The store also sold robots. The electronic controllers were provided and you could add accessories to create different looks with attachable arms legs and a wide selection of heads. This was anther shop that Jody marked down to revisit as soon as his allowance was available hoping that next year he would be getting a raise. He'd need one after all the items he'd seen today. Maybe mom has an employee discount or a son of an employee discount.

Next stop was a store called *Skulls*. It resembled a museum except that all the heads and bones were copies of real fossils making them accessible to everyone who didn't happen to have several millions of dollars available for purchases. A customer was negotiating for a Tyrannosaurs Rex with very sharp teeth, and was told that would be a special order and would take about a week. Kacy thought this place was a little creepy but Jody was intrigued by the replica skulls of Buffalo, Long Horn cattle (perfect for over a hunting lodge fireplace),

Wildcats, Coyotes, and even Smilodons which were prehistoric sabre tooth cats. With their wide open mouths to accommodate their six inch incisors they appeared to always be laughing. Jody tried out a simple joke and yep she was laughing.

Kacy was more attracted to *Yore Toys* the operative word being toys, a store which featured all classic toys such as Yo Yo's, Cabbage Patch Kids, doll's houses, Tinker Toys, Cats-eye marbles and early versions of action figures, pinball machines and pogo sticks. A Mr. Potato Head had a prime display spot, only fitting for the first toy that was ever advertised on television. They both soon lost interest though because none of the toys were digital or interactive. For the best as most of these toys which originally sold for a few dollars were now often worth in the thousands to collectors.

They passed by an internet café without going in because after all they had computers at home. Inside the café they saw the front half of two men in a deer suit typing away while the back half relaxed on a chair. In another booth what appeared to be a Santa's elf was typing at superfast speed, the fastest they had ever seen, while at the same time surreptitiously intent on surveying the deer's keystrokes. Or maybe they were just imaging that.

# XII

*G*OLD had been discovered in Raspberry creek in the 1800's. It was that immortal cry. There's gold in them thar hills! Not those hills. Them thar ones!

Gold had also been the motivation for exploration several hundred years earlier when the Spaniards had journeyed north after looting the treasures of the ancient kingdoms they had found in the new world. There had to be more gold to be had and there were stories of a city of gold somewhere in this area. Two old worlds had collided, ironically each one of them thinking the other was new and there followed tragic consequences which carried down even to present day. But they found no cities, just never ending plains with giant herds of Buffalo and the bones of other creatures five times their size with incredibly sharp teeth, which is why they kept a secure watch at night in case these behemoths returned from their grazing grounds which they guessed were further north. It hadn't occurred to them that these animals were extinct as evolution had not as yet been realized. They thought the monsters might be hiding somewhere, at the bottom of lakes or in secret valleys. Their sanctuaries were the basis of many fables mostly invented to scare children from wandering off alone or swimming out too far.

Much of this had been predicted by a medicine woman or dream lady, a Shaman who had a way with animals and medicinal herbs, and looked into the future through smoke dreams. As such she was a highly respected member of the local tribes.

On the other side of the world in the very same time period, but in a different time zone, women who talked to animals, created healing potions or predicted the future were being put to the stake. Scientists were not common in this age but some would shine immortal, their theories outliving most prophesies. These men were rare, thinking outside the prevailing boxes and some were accused of heresy in the days where faith spat in the face of reason, a perpetual battle where science eventually proved more lenient and more mannerly. Even Nostradamus who wasn't just a future seer but a scientist delving into chemical properties of substances and the causes of disease was criticized. He knew nothing of our dream lady even though they were in the same profession, but then she didn't know about him either, so there.

They came as foreseen, the bearded ones with the

smoking weapons. First by river in keelboats and canoes then by land on magnificent animals with flowing manes and tails. They came like the water, one drop, then another then a trickle ...!

These Europeans had made the false assumption that this new continent they had arrived to was essentially empty of human life, not realizing that many, many varied groups of inhabitants had called it their home over thousands of years each displacing the other in turn. After a few months traversing the area all they had discovered was a few rudimentary weapons stashed here and there by some unseen locals. Their current owners being absent, the Spanish commander was prompted to make a fatal mistake in the tradition of the world's oldest profession, the souvenir business. "I wonder how this spear would look in my den." Any person that sets foot in medicine country, even today, knows they are on consecrated ground. The spirits are there and all they ask for is a little respect. Search parties found only one survivor of the expedition and all he could utter was Phantasmas.

This event was the beginning of the rumors that the hill was possessed and sensible folks gave it a wide berth. Later, in the westward expansion era wagon trains of settlers had passed through this land as quickly as possible on their way west. Some brought grape vine cuttings with them hoping to grow grapes and make wine once they reached their destination which they would ultimately achieve. Others had brought garden variety plants, mint, sage, oregano to spice up their very bland cooking. Some had brought apple seeds, but that's another story, and a few had brought raspberry plants.

A wagon train was like a leper crawling across the plains. As he crawled pieces of him kept dropping off. From one raspberry bush came a field, seeds scattered to the four winds and the raspberry plants began to grow unabated. For many years after Raspberry Hill had been pretty much left to the tumbleweeds and coyotes, hundreds of them howling at the moon the way dogs howl to music. To the locals this was all earth's beautiful blanket, the tumbleweeds and the lonely coyotes were part of this patchwork along with the moon and the stars and their music was as sweet as Aunt Maggie's lullabies. For the newcomers it struck a different chord. These Coyotes and prairie Wolves and their obsessive wailing scared children and tenderfeet into thinking the hill was spooked. On windy nights the sound was bone chilling. The lessons of European folklore they carried with them ran deep. Animals weren't the only creatures that bayed at midnight. Eventually the coyotes were run off except for the most stubborn ones, and what is now a freeway was once called Coyote Pass.

As word had spread of the gold discovery, a makeshift

town grew up on the hill almost overnight, and before long this country was swarming with the great unwashed, the lure of gold far outweighing any fear of bad or even good magic. What gold they found was mostly squandered on the usual wild west pursuits, whiskey, women, and gambling, and any attempts at a civilized way of life did not take root because marriageable women were in short supply. The reasons for this were obvious. Strolling down the street in any frontier town you would find smelly saloons, poker parlors, blacksmiths, mangy flop houses, saddle makers, corals, gunsmiths and one general store. Only one place in five hundred square miles to buy a dress or a new hat, and usually from a catalog allowing four to six months for delivery. Conditions were intolerable: There was nowhere to shop!

Then the gold that was easy to access in the rivers and streams was panned out. Almost as quickly as it had appeared the town all but disappeared as the prospectors moved on to the next strike, the average age of boomtowns being three years. Oh there was still some gold there and silver, but buried deep in the ground and would require years of actual work to dig it up.

Gangs of rustlers and bank robbers risked any possibility of otherworldly inhabitants and started using the place as a hideout but as the west became tamed the place again fell into oblivion because these same outlaws were either killed off or became respectable businessmen building large farms and ranches hoping to turn their boney cows into fat herds and their boney sons into cattle barons.

In the twenties the rickety town became a notorious truck stop because all the trucks were loaded with booze, the new liquid gold. Bootleggers also appreciated the view up here because they could see in all directions which was important if you were breaking the law. It has been said that some of their associates were buried up here, as were most of their competitors. Eventually prohibition was repealed and what had been labeled The Noble Experiment or The Failed Experiment depending on your point of view was over. Later in the late thirties and early forties the hill was pretty much ignored and deserted, the entire world being full of very bad medicine at that time.

Throughout this entire history of this place there were many unresolved land ownership disputes. Whose desolate land was it anyway? The earliest known inhabitants were perhaps the large beasts with the sharp teeth. Ultimately, no surprise, it was claimed by the US government. Then Air Conditioning was invented.

WHEN MACINTOSH CAME ALONG, being a visionary, he could immediately see the possibilities and his idea for Raspberry Hill Mall was born. He purchased the hill at what appeared to be an exorbitant price but in the long view was a complete bargain.

The best businessmen and gamblers say that money is a tool, but to Macintosh it seemed more like a toy. He did things differently, not following any prescribed rules yet always being super successful sparking rumors often fueled by jealousy along the way. A lot of billionaires keep low profiles but not this low. Magazines and newspapers all followed their own leads to try to uncover his origins and even an underground newspaper headquartered at the top of an urban skyscraper was working an angle. A couple of papers even joined together in their search which was unheard of. So far it was all conjecture. Macintosh was everything from a mobster to the prodigal son of a sheik. One paper suggested that he was a member of British royalty and another thought he might be the frontman for a conglomerate of Japanese movie stars. Then there was the notion that he wasn't a human being at all, but a dead tycoon's pet cat. (According to one expert more estates are left to cats than any other animal.) Lastly was the idea, a not too far out one, that Macintosh had actually found that fabled city of gold as he seemed to have a never ending supply of funds at his disposal. Perhaps if they had examined the records of the M Mining Company many of their questions would have been answered.

# XIII

*O*ld Tombstone, another mall minicourt, was replete with cowboys in full western dress and even a few cows wandering the streets. Sage brushes swirled helplessly like big city cowgirls in a genuine sandstorm. Here as in most cowboy movies all was dust, so where were the grassy plains for the cows to graze on we might wonder. The main street Allen Street, was lined with souvenir shops and the inevitable honkeytonk. From inside could be heard showtunes and music from all the great western Broadway shows and film soundtracks playing at just the right volume to be conducive to shopping. Several restaurants featured BBQ ribs beans and bacon, each proclaiming their recipes to be the most authentically from the old west.

*Stablemates* featured his and her western clothing and *Boot Hill* sold cowboy boots, of course, but also belts, saddles and bridles, everything for the avid horseperson. Next to them was a western cigar store *Peace Pipe Bobs* complete with a cigar store Indian by the front door. This was actually Bob himself, a local Indian who liked to pose for photos with his patrons earning more from these photos than from the Turquoise Indian jewelry, tobacco, accessories and nick-nacks for sale inside the store. Actually he was a day trader. From his office in the back his photo earnings went to good use as he worked the stock market to his favor for fun and profit.

At one end was the Marshall's office where the town Marshall, from Sarge's security crew in full lawman's outfit, sat on his porch whittling. The OK Corral at the other end was the location for mock gunfight shows, realistic but harmless because they used squirt guns, so it was also rated OK for families to enter since it promoted very little violence, unlike the real old west that reeked of it. Jack and Jody entered a roping contest but Kacy was focused on only one thing. Where there are cowboys there have to be horses. And there were. Horse rides were available but the line was far too long for them to wait it out. Jack pointed out the mechanical horse rides and bull rides but Kacy stubbornly was only interested in real horse rides.

THEY PROCEEDED BACK INTO the main mall. "Next we will go from the old frontier to the new frontier" said Jack

"but I need to let you know there will be no horses here."
The entranceway was marked *Space Concourse*. Kacy
knew when she was being catered to. "Of course not silly,
everyone knows there are no horses in space." Macintosh
had created this section in conjunction with NASA who
could always rely on him to donate millions as needed
since space exploration was another of his passions. His
philosophy was that the universe is expanding and the
Macintosh corporation planned to expand with it.

Along the walls displays covered the history of
flight from long ago when the Chinese had invented
tiny helicopters as children's toys to replicas of landers
and extraterrestrial vehicles currently in use. Photos
of all the astronauts past and present lined the walls,
their smiling faces belying the extreme dangers they
faced. You could view all the previous space launches and
landings on a bank of viewing screens in chronological
order. Beautifully rendered star charts and maps with
both ancient and modern names were laid out on light
tables along with new and classical measuring devices.
Models of Da Vinci's flying machine and the Wright
Brothers first airplane hung from the ceiling along with
hot air balloons used in previous centuries for tourism
and inevitably for battles and spying as demonstrated
in the American Civil war. Inventions have often been
co-opted for military use as that was where the funding
for innovations usually came from. Macintosh believed

in pure research and was doing his part to keep space as a peaceful place, fingers crossed. There was even a small section promoting the best Science fiction writers and shows which although loosely based on science sometimes had amazing accuracy in predicting scientific inventions, while some were just complete trash.

They climbed into a scaled down Mars rover which drove them past launch rockets and through mock up villages showing what daily life would be like on other planets and finally over 3D flooring making you feel like you were in orbit around an incredible planet. Signs pointed to the entrances of the planetarium and the space observatory but since our trio didn't have enough for the required entrance fees they decided to revisit on another day. At the exit was information on how to participate in this grand space adventure by selecting a career in science, technology and engineering. Jody had always wanted to become a reporter like his dad but now this opened possibilities. Maybe he could become the first real space reporter, not just a communications officer relating facts but someone with language skills that could ride along in the rockets to report and explain events in literary terms to the people back on earth hopefully in his daydream winning a Pulitzer in the process.

CONTINUING THEIR TOUR THEY entered *Three Cord Wonders*. It was a music store with guitars and drums in the window display that would automatically appeal to young would-be musicians to visit inside. Jody was no exception. There was a recording studio, a demo room and you could sign up for lessons at all levels. When asked at award ceremonies who had supported and encouraged them in their careers a preponderance of musicians would give credit to their mothers (or grandmothers). Even now a young man was on his knees playing wildly in his best rock star pose, showing his mother his progression so far in order to encourage her to purchase the more expensive guitar. Wistfully day dreaming of the house he would one day buy for her she relented. The store had everything music, from stage lights, mixing boards and equalizers to tuning forks, original vinyl, cd's and audio tapes. The selections represented all categories and technologies from the beginnings of recording time to the present day thanks to Edison or was it Tesla.

Strange how songs once banned from the radio were now played at major sporting events. The devil's music of yesteryear is now shopping music complete with synthesized violins replacing guitars, many with the offensive lyrics removed, (America being so sensitive these days that this often meant all the lyrics) proving that if you are patient enough you just might come into mainstream vogue. How must composers feel whose blood sweat and creative tears are now used to sell everything from chicken sandwiches to designer underwear. "Far out man, just send the check."

"Mom and dad love music, lets get them some Christmas music as an extra present." offered Kacy. "Great idea we'll do that as soon as we get our next allowance." responded Jody. Saved by lack of funds. Neither of them knew that after hearing Christmas music all day every day for over a month the last thing Parlett needed was more. If she heard one more chestnut roasting on one more open fire she would start screaming.

Chocolate shops were located in several locations in the mall and have you noticed that they are usually built out with white tiles possibly to make the creamy dark chocolate stand out. Kacy wanted to go inside but they were the kids that stayed out of the candy store as they now were pretty much broke and these stores were a little pricey for the average person mostly appealing to ladies purchasing chocolate delicacies for special occasions for get togethers and parties. Romance novel authors often participated in chocolate festivals at the mall as nibbling on chocolate seemed to make reading their books more fun. Even vampire romance novelists capitalized on this by featuring red raspberry chocolate. One writer had a series on vampire presidents skipping some and starting with Adams. Washington had bad teeth possibly from eating too much chocolate so he could only gum you in the neck so that edition was a non starter.

They made their way to the rides and amusement floor since it was not overly crowded, and buy one get one free rides were being offered as the day evolved, since most shoppers were frantically focused on shopping now determined to obtain all the last minute goods they could. Kacy rode the carousel on an ostrich that slowly revolved around a bank of mirrors. Macintosh had scoured the countryside procuring bits and bobs of original merry-go-rounds gleaned from defunct state fairgrounds and amusement parks. Experts refurbished and assembled these treasures until the beautiful Raspberry Hill carousel emerged, a classic showpiece conjuring slower more carefree times. Other choices of seats were camels, lions and tigers, penguins and beautifully carved horses which Kacy refused to ride holding out for a real horse that she instinctively knew had to be around here somewhere. The two boys naturally were fascinated by the *Raspberry Whip* a berry-go-round thrill ride with spinning raspberries. Outside speakers were positioned so that the people in line could hear the passengers screaming causing them to want to take the ride all the more. This was one of those vein bursting, death by hemorrhage rides guaranteed to raise your adrenaline to the boiling point. When they disembarked from the Whip their faces were white and drained but being boys they had to pretend they were just fine, even suggesting that they should all try the roller-coaster next. This was designed as a giant Chinese dragon perpetually chasing it's tail and breathing fire as it ascended and descended loop after impossible loop. Kacy never opened her eyes once, thankful they were both with her and tightly gripped their hands until that ride was over.

## XIV

*C*hrissy's assignments for today were starting to
make her feel a little heavyheaded and it was getting later. She decided that she had set too high a goal
for herself and she would have to select a few more stores
to visit and mail the rest of the rental notices. We have
a Post Office located here so we might as well use it she
reasoned. After all anyone visiting this mall could spend
a full week and still not see everything offered so there
was no way she would ever have enough time to visit
every store in one day. If only Gatewood had helped
distribute the letters a lot more would have been accom-
plished but she hadn't even laid eyes on him today and
when she had arrived at *Putter's Island* at the direction
of Flora he was long gone. To where she had no idea. Her
musings were interrupted by the appearance of Elsie her
little wagon in tow. "Hello Chrissy, you look like you
could use a cup of tea. Park you car here and come with
me." Curious Parlett followed her through a door marked
'Storeroom' into a concealed elevator that functioned like
a pneumatic tube and moments later she found herself

at doors opening on a penthouse apartment, an aerie with a view overlooking the entire mall.

It was richly furnished in new furniture custom made to appear antique. In one corner was a very large TV screen which upon closer examination was also connected to a computer. Like many in the mall Parlett had previously assumed that Elsie was a half crazy bag lady but this attic was impeccable. Antique leatherbound books and a Baby Grand Piano completed the décor. Various magazines were strewn on a coffee table constructed to look like a giant book. She glanced at the mailing labels on the magazines and now it all became clear. "So Macintosh is your...?" She asked. "Yes my son and he takes excellent care of his mother." And Gatewood is your..?" "My grandson, Macintosh's sister's son. Please relax your job is quite secure. You are doing excellent work and we are all pulling for you here. Alexander has a lot of growing up to do. He was nice as a child but since his uncle's unqualified success he has gotten off track and he doesn't realize that success comes only with hard work and following fair practices and not just because he has a relative that is good at business. He needs a good jolt in the ... to set him straight."

She continued "I honestly don't know where my son's business acumen springs from. I was a school teacher and my husband, his father was a surgeon. In fact that is how we met. My friends had been insisting that I go ice skating with them. I didn't really want to go but they kept coercing me until I finally relented and gave in. After a few unsteady circuits on the ice I tripped and twisted my ankle and he was the young doctor that patched me back up. It was a twist of fate. Do you believe in love at first sight?" "Yes unequivocally." responded Chrissy. She remembered how she and Chick had ridden the school bus together everyday since grade school because they had lived just a mile away from each other in the mountains. Then they had dated through high school. "In college my husband and I studied English literature. How that prepared me to be a mall manager is anyone's guess but it seems to be working. It does seem that we were meant for each other whether people believe in that sort of thing or they don't."

Elsie brought out the Tea. "Old Barbosa my favorite." Chrissy continued the conversation. "Do you play?" she asked pointing to the piano. "Oh yes replied Elsie "I even won various competitions in my youth." "And is your computer tied into the mall's mainframe?" "Yes but I don't use it much. I prefer to shop in person because then everything fits me better. Jack uses it for his classes." "Who is Jack?" "My fairy godson." OK maybe Elsie was a bit crazy. "I had no idea this apartment was in the mall, who else visits here?" "My husband visits me occasionally to check on me even though he is gone now. That's another thing, Gatewood thinks I should be in a home because he has no imagination or belief in the unknowable. Also my sewing club visits," she said gesturing to the antique dressmaker's dummy next to a large wardrobe, "and sometimes the elves." "The Santa's elves visit you here?" "Not those posers, there are real elves living here haven't you seen them? I advise them on important issues and in return they make sure all the plants in the mall are receiving proper care which they seem to excel at. My son doesn't know about them and I'm afraid that if I tell him he wont allow them to stay. So it's a secret. Can you keep it?" More than a bit crazy Chrissy decided. There is a fine line between fantasy and reality and Elsie was playing jumprope with that line. Elves indeed! Time to go she decided, that was enough craziness for today, so be kind and humor her fantasies. "Of course I can Elsie. Thanks for the tea and now I must resume my rounds. I have a lot more shops to visit today. See you at the Christmas Party later?"

After the very interesting and enlightening afternoon tea bordering on a Mad Hatter's Teaparty, Chrissy reset her goals and feeling much better started to drive the little car really fast, much faster than the 5 mph speed limit posted throughout the mall. Hopkins was right, this little car is more fun, but I cant even think about keeping it, the payments would stretch out over 50 years! The real purpose of the posted speed limit was to prevent skate boarding, roller-skating and roller blading which could have resulted in shoppers getting knocked about. Lost in her thoughts she was definitely speeding and consequently an eager security guard pulled her over. "You were exceeding the speed limit." "So, what do we do now? Are you taking me downtown?" Parlett was enjoying the exchange because she knew that in her costume, unless alerted, people would not know who she was. "Don't get smart with me lady. Where'd you get this car anyway? I think you had better visit the security office. My superiors will get to the bottom of this."

"Speaking of your superiors here comes one now. Hello Sarge, I'm being arrested." She winked. "Good afternoon Ms. Parlett I see you have met Corporal Cooper soon to be Private Cooper. Congratulations Cooper you have just put the collar on our commander in chief, so you'd better put away the handcuffs." adding to Parlett "please cut him some slack he's just a rookie, first week on the job. I have a number of new hires brought in to beef up our staff for the holidays." "Well there was no harm done, let him off with a warning this time" she said as she restarted the car and drove off at 15 mph. "I owe you one Sarge." said Cooper. "Good You just volunteered for the night shift."

As PARLETT DROVE INTO the entrance to Chinaville, one of the international minicourts, she was almost sideswiped by an electric rickshaw also disobeying the speed limit.

She made a note that one of those, though not as roomy, might be a possible replacement for her electric car. She would have to return it to Hopkins eventually, as his purchase price was out of the question, and she wasn't looking forward to driving her bland golf cart again.

This China town was representative of the old China as if the revolution had never happened or never been televised, televisions being symbols of western decadence. She headed to *The Silk Road* a clothing shop which sold silk pajamas. Many people had the general idea from the movies that all Chinese people wore clothing resembling pajamas. Being capitalists at heart, instead of taking offense, the proprietors of this store had monetized this misconception specializing in actual silk pajamas and loungewear, casual attire for long winter evenings while watching television. Chrissy selected a matched pair for herself and Chick hoping to replace his smoking jacket since the very word smoking often prompted him to want a cigarette.

This minicourt also functioned as a Chinese cultural center with art and antiquity galleries, calligraphy classes and a language school. Next to the chinese grocery store with imported staples and delicacies was a series of americanized oriental restaurants, mung beans on the boil, featuring cuisine from all parts of China from Mongolia to Peking. but Parlett had no time for snicksnacks now except perhaps a fortune cookie from the stand by the exit that sold both fortune and misfortune cookies, your choice. Even the misfortune cookies usually had somewhat optimistic messages so as not to be a threat to the patrons' good humor. She opened her fortune cookie and read. *You will meet a stranger. A cute little fellow. He will show you the way.* Her misfortune cookie read Your mailman is stealing your coupons. (Actually Fortune cookies originated in Japan not China but most people didn't know this.)

Next on Parlett's list was *Amelia Bloomers* a ladies underwear store. Amelia had advocated bloomers in the 1800's so that ladies could ride bicycles and not get their dresses caught in the wheels and spokes. Then on to *Clodhoppers*, the very latest in footwear. A giant talking shoe at the entrance greeting patrons was overheard to quietly mutter "Your mama wears combat boots" at least that is what it sounded like to Parlett. That's not right, another malfunction she was sure and she made a note of it as they were starting to really add up. She purchased their newest item, slipper socks that looked like a pair of loafers perfect for comfort for a long day at the office. After she had placed an order for some other items at both shops to be sent over to her apartment she realized that she was quickly becoming her own best customer. Good thing she had an employee discount.

*The Man Cave* up ahead was a reminder that besides presents for herself she needed to pick up a few more items to surprise Chick in case he wasn't thrilled with the silk pajamas. He didn't need a BBQ Grill as they had access to all the best restaurants in the mall, so why grill! Maybe some specialty hot sauce, this store sold almost fifty varieties. She didn't care for it but he spread it on everything ever since they had vacationed in New Orleans, visiting a hot sauce factory that among other spices the air was saturated with salt to the point they were both weeping alligator tears as they left. She considered a motorized tie rack but Chick would only wear a tie when he absolutely had to. How about a spear or a suit of armor. Totally useless but it might look good in his den. She settled on an indoor marshmallow roaster so they could pretend to be camping out while staying in.

Lastly the Wedding Chapel was doing an exceptional business judging by the queue lined up outside. It was located next to a flower shop, a bridal shop and a jewelry store for convenience of the customers. ID's were checked at the door making sure you weren't too young but the older customers were waved right through because apparently you were never too old. Instant matrimony, five minutes and out. Fortunately the wedding certificates came with annulment papers that could be easily filed in case the joy of the season wore off later in the day. Most of these weddings stuck though, because there is someone out there for everyone, if you are willing to take that risk.

XV

*The Irish Pub* was her next destination after finally completing the remaining store visits she had selected. Parlett arrived there for an appointment to meet with the Santa's Elves Union's representatives because they had brought their lawyer to renegotiate their contract for the following year. This pub was a favorite gathering place for store employees at the end of the day and also for shoppers with sore feet. All such places were located near the exits so as to minimize on tipsy shoppers wandering through the mall. She noticed Scipio the puppeteer at a corner table holding court with a lively group who were half snockered and still in their Santa's elves costumes. There had been plenty of elves at Santa's Palace and now here were more elves merrymaking during business hours. "Make a note, did we over hire?" she added to today's recorded comments so she could review them later.

Unions and labor organizations are important for any working person promoting safe workplaces and equitable pay, but occasionally their demands are too extreme. Thanks to collective bargaining these union members also portrayed cupids for Valentine's day, Leprechauns for St Patrick's Day, and any other event that required diminutive people. The union's new contract specified more pay, less hours and more benefits. No problem there as she was all for that, but for some reason they also wanted to pick their own Santa Claus (too extreme). So she asked. "And why do you feel we should have a different Santa? Our current Santa is recognized universally as the best Santa ever." "You are right." was the reply. "He may well be the best in the business as he says, that is not the issue. Because this Santa spends a lot of time promoting himself in the media and in TV interviews telling everyone he is the penultimate in his field. Five interviews in the past three days. As a group portraying elves we work diligently towards the overall Santa experience and would just like to occasionally be included in these TV and radio promotions We asked him to include some Santa's elves on these shows at least twice and he turned us down. The man has turned into an egomaniac wishing to keep the spotlight firmly placed on himself,"

"So it's just about not being on television that is upsetting you? I will happily speak with him about this on your behalf." "Good luck with that. A one hundred and fifty foot high tech tree seems to threaten everyone's opinion of himself so what value can a few Santa's helpers have to him by comparison." "As your mall manager I think I have a little clout and I believe I can rectify this, I just wish you had brought this to my attention earlier." "We did discuss this with Mr. Gatewood and his response was just to give us the afternoon off, nice but not a solution." To cinch their argument they thought they had a foolproof bargaining chip. "A Santa Claus you can find just about anywhere, but elves are hard to come by!" Their additional leverage was to remind her that when Easter arrived she would be needing someone to climb into the little rabbit suits. "Hmmmm. Maybe this Easter we'll use Giant Rabbits!! Look guys I promise to resolve this personally just not in this formal agreement. Compromise is the marriage of opposing viewpoints." It's an old saying but old sayings are for people who cant come up with new ones. After a little more haggling back and forth Chrissy scratched out the Claus clause and signed and initialed the contract.

"Scipio get in the car, the mall is closing soon, time to go. Why do I feel like a designated driver." she said after picking up Scipio's tab which turned out to be rather hefty since he had included the Santa's elves tab with his own. "Grazi Cristina" he mumbled. Chrissy had taken Scipio under her wing because her kids loved him. He had performed a couple of puppet shows at their birthday parties and she felt drawn to his eccentric personality and like most women she believed she could cure him of his bad habits which were notable. Once when he was doing a charity gig in a retirement home she had to get him released because the well meaning attendants had refused to let him leave thinking he was a slightly inebriated resident. "This car and your costume brings back memories." Mused Scipio. "My little old grandmother had a car exactly like this. She would pick me up from school and take me for my favorite ice cream, Pistachio. Then we would go to the beach. She would swim laps around the lighthouse while I strolled along the shore collecting driftwood to make puppets. She was training for the senior Olympics but never won. Too many ice cream cones."

They headed up an elevator toward the entrance to the EL which connected the mall to the six star hotel *La Framboisier* where many of the performers stayed along with shoppers and visitors. As if the mall wasn't visitor worthy enough this hotel was a comfortable masterpiece, both in architecture and accoutrements. The lobby was furnished in ultra modern Scandinavian furniture and in the center was the world's largest chandelier. (Everything connected with Raspberry Hill had to be the world's largest and as soon as it wasn't Macintosh ordered something new that was.) The windows on every side overlooked expansive views and on the walls there were more rare paintings from Macintosh's collection. Permanent employees including Chrissy and her family lived in the spacious apartments adjacent and connected to the hotel through the lobby with access to all the hotels features, including several world class restaurants and an indoor pool and tennis courts.

The EL entrance was like a subway station but in the sky. A series of lighted rounded pods, each seating up to six, dangled from immense cables giving the illusion of a giant string of multicolored Christmas lights which transversed the enormous parking lot now heavily covered in snow with more gently falling. Purple and white snowflakes shimmered in the whirlpool of fresh air and mall air as the pod bay door opened like Sesame, Ali Baba's pet rock. Each pod was glass bottomed and the entire shell was photosensitive, tinting and untinting, to sunlight and moonlight. New Age music, light and watery, or Krell music as some described it, was piped in to give the feeling of traveling in a bubble. It was an amazing piece of technology right down to the pushbutton or verbally operated spacesickness bag dispensary at the side, just in case. In broad daylight the unaided eye could take in the entire metropolis all the way to the airport and the farmland in the next county. Besides the direct route to the hotel there was an auxiliary branch that circled the entire mall. For anyone with an hour to kill it was a stunning experience. On a clear night while drifting in a pod with stars above and the city lights in the distance, imagining yourself in a spaceport wasn't far flung. Outside their pod the only noise was the patting of snowflakes, huge and perfectly formed as if they were cut out of crepe paper by kindergartners. The snow was far too deep now and it was too late for the outdoor ski slope and the toboggan and sled slopes to be open, but tomorrow once the snow stopped the cries and squeals of delight would echo over the vastness.

Below a lone figure wearing an alpine hat, a faux fur coat, mukluks and with what appeared to be snowshoes trudged through the snow. Looking over the largest parking lot in the world Parlett could only think of one thing, The mind boggling fortune it would cost in two years when it needed to be resurfaced.

Using the touchpad in the pod Parlett flicked off the lights so they could better appreciate the view. The entire apparatus came to a grinding halt. "Now what?" So many things going wrong today it couldn't be a coincidence. First the fog machine then the escalators now this. "Don't worry it will reboot and fix itself shortly." She reassured the nervous Scipio who was eyeing the bag dispensary.

Scipio kept his prized puppets in mahogany trunks,

quite valuable themselves. Like real actors they all had names apart from the characters they played. Scipio had loaded a smallish trunk onto the EL. "What's in the Trunk?" "One of my favorite children Luigi. (He referred to his puppets as his children.) He may play Scrooge but he's a real nice guy. I'm taking him back to my room to repair him. He's usually fit as a violin but one of his strings is loose." Parlett had always suspected that more than one of Scipio's strings was loose. "By the way it's fit as a fiddle." "Did you see my show tonight?" She nodded " Scipio how do you do it?" "Do what signora?" "Make the puppet ghost drink the milk," "It's not real milk, it's a trick glass." He showed her. 'Turn it up and the glass empties, set it down and it fills up again. Now I need you to answer a question for me and be totally honest. Hold nothing back, I am Scipio with nerves of steel. Could you see the strings?"

XVI

*The Movie theater* is where the kids were heading now and adjacent to it was a shop and snackbar called *The Two Bit Movie Museum and Grill.* The items within proved that the proprietor had a slightly offbeat sense of humor or just not enough funds to purchase more spectacular items. As they walked through the guide explained. "There's the sport jacket James Dean wore in Rebel Without A Cause." "I thought he wore a leather jacket" said Jack. "He did but that was later on. When you first see him he was wearing this sport jacket." Next was the Tin Man's oil can, the sodapop bottle Shane brought back for the deposit, the bullet used to kill Old Yeller, the dance charts from To Sir With Love, a jar of soup made from Rodan's birdsnest, a bed sheet from The Exorcist, Sydney Greenstreet's fly-swatter from Casablanca, Esther William's nose plugs, a plumber's bob with the three marks of Arne Sacnusem, a bottle of sand from Iwo Jima, Motel's spools of thread from Fiddler On The Roof, the pine cone Julie Andrews sat on in The Sound Of Music and the unfaithful wife's braids from The Vikings, just to name a few.

Each artifact came with an authenticating photograph from the original movie. The place of honor was occupied by Ben Hur's oar, the one he was chained to, Stanley Kowalski's bowling ball, and James Coburn's switchblade from The Magnificent Seven which was totally unique since switchblades weren't invented until 1933.

This was all lost on Kacy and Jody as they had seen none of these movies, but Jack being a movie lover with plenty of time on his hands had gone to every retro film festival the theater periodically held.

The *Raspberry Hill Multiplex* had twenty screens with enough variety of shows to tear even the most jaded filmgoer away from their television set two point five times a year on average. Seventy percent of all out-of-towners visiting the mall took in a movie. One peek into the leviathan lobby and they were sucked in like plankton. Macintosh had made sure this theater was constructed like the theater palaces of old but also fully modernized. Locations with classic names like The Rialto, The Majestic, The Granada, and The Orpheum which still exist in many cities were copied down to the minutest detail. The ceiling above was emblazoned with stars emitting a soft light that complemented the gold ornate carvings swathed in velvet drapes below. Inside the theater the trio settled into their seats 3D glasses and popcorn in hand. The ticket taker had waved them through without paying as he owed Jack a favor. The state of the art seating allowed adjustments similar to a recliner, so comfortable, causing more than a few patrons to doze off during performances. That is what happened to our little trio, their wanderings having tuckered them out and they fell asleep before the Blob consumed the entire theater. When they awoke their theater was completely dark and empty, the cleanup people having been allowed to leave early so they could attend the Christmas party. Worse than that the electronic gate was down trapping them in the lobby, leaving no way out until suddenly and mysteriously it lifted on it's own for a few feet, just high enough for them to scoot under.

"Mom is not answering her phone" said Jody. "We need to find a security guard." There were none to be seen and in fact the mall seemed completely empty and very quiet. Jack was worried as he knew from experience that usually at this time of night the janitorial crews would be playing music at full blast as they cleaned and polished. Time for an alternate plan. He led them over to an expresscalator, an elevator that could only be operated by a special key which was attached to his belt loop, and they zoomed up to the twenty first floor which was the mall's attic. " This is my friend Elsie's apartment" explained Jack. They entered her penthouse at the top but no Elsie. There was a note on the kitchen table. "Jack dear I'll be at the Christmas party if you need me. There's pizza for dinner in the fridge if you want to heat it up." "Now what?" said Jody not worried for himself but for the little sister he was supposed to be watching out for. "Follow me I know what to do." said Jack as he opened the doors of a large armoire in a corner against the wall next to a grand piano. "Step inside." "It's just like Narnia." bubbled Kacy. "Will there be a lion on the other side?" Jack laughed. "That's in a storybook, this is just a door." and he proceeded to knock.

After a few moments the door was opened by a four foot tall elf holding a bag of marshmallows. "Well hello Jack, welcome, how was the movie, you look hungry, bring your friends, we are roasting hot dogs, meat or turkey if you prefer." A group of elves seated around a very large fireplace hung with size small socks, were busily rotating sticks and cheering each time a marshmallow burst into flames. The entire attic was bathed in candlelight from the many decorative candles large and small adding to the jolly scene. Apparently the elves were regular customers of the candle shop as many of the candles had the Clover's trademark perfumes rendering the entire loft overpoweringly sweet and dreamy. "We need help finding their parents." said Jack gesturing toward Jody and Kacy. "I'm afraid they have gotten lost somewhere below." "Well let's take a look. Don't worry I know every nook and cranny in this mall." said Zeeke leading them to a wall of windows looking down on all twenty floors providing an overview of many of the stores and shops. He opened a door to an observation desk complete with telescopes the kind used for looking upwards at the stars. Zeeke aimed one downwards. "The only movement I can see is the dog catcher rounding up stray dogs and placing them in his van. I don't see your family yet so why don't you join us by the fire and we'll keep checking until we see them."

Jody had questions. He wanted to know who these people were and he proceeded to question them imitating his dad's best interviewing manner. "Are you just visiting or do you live here like Jack?" "Yes to both" replied Zeeke, who apparently was the leader and spokesperson for the group. "We are astronomers and the mall is an ideal place for viewing the stars since we are high enough up to avoid the distortion from city lights giving us an almost perfect vantage point. I can show you some of the detailed star maps and charts we have made. Have you visited the planetarium and observatory yet? They're some of our favorite places and we attend wonderful parties during galactic events, eclipses, meteor showers, supernovas."

"Are you magic elves?" asked Kacy hopefully. "Ah magic," Zeeke paused, "there are magic tricks and then there is magic. It is magic that we exist in this vast universe and because we are made of the building blocks of stars, magic is present in all of us." he concluded cryptically. He liked these human children and of course Jack who he had known for several months now, but he wasn't prepared to divulge the elves' secrets as that would go against the code. He ushered them to another part of the attic where colorful plants and flowers were growing in fantastical flower beds filling the air with the luxurious perfumes they were emitting. "We are also naturalists and horticulturists, so besides our own gardens here there is an unlimited variety of plants at the mall to study and catalog." "Well you must be good gardeners because I've never seen these plants and flowers this large before" commented Jody staring at forget-me-nots as tall as rose bushes, roses the size of dessert bowls and heads of lettuce as large as watermelons. "That's because we give them special care and it could be something in the water" replied Zeeke not wishing to reveal any more details. Against the far wall was bookshelf after bookshelf loaded with all manner of publications. Some just cloth bound others bound in leather with gilded lettering. Jody was amazed. "Where did you get so many books?" "We have collected these over the years and bring them along wherever we go. There's nothing like a good book to help pass the afternoon or evening, reading them is very relaxing." Then he went on to share some of the elves' history and even Jody, always the sceptic, was starting to be convinced that elves really did exist and that he was in their presence.

Zeeke introduced them to his wife Bee who was arranging buns, mustard and relish on a platter for when the hot dogs were nice and crispy from the fire. She took Kacy's hand and led her and Jack over to the fireplace to join the happy group that were now alternately singing carols and relating stories of their many past adventures, which naturally became more improvised and exaggerated as each elf tried to outdo their companions. The elves loved storytelling and many of the stories were real but they always admitted which ones were made up at the end and then they would burst into laughter. In fact they laughed a lot which seemed to be a reflection of their excellent good nature.

Against one wall there were three elves seated at computer terminals. One of them was the elf they had seen earlier in the internet café. "What are they doing, web surfing, shopping?" asked Jody. "They are fixing things. They are not connected to the internet they are connected to the mall's intranet. You need to understand that like the futuristic city of Diaspar the mall and surrounding buildings in this complex are one big machine. One hacker in Mongolia could turn the biggest shopping mall into a little shop of horrors or more appropriately a big one. Whomever manages to log in controls all the functions in the mall. We have discovered that there are serious flaws in the current system mostly because of overreliance on automated (or artificial) intelligence. The person who did the original programming obviously excels in their field however computers are just a box, albeit a huge one but to keep things safe we need to think outside the box which requires human intervention or in our case non human intervention. It has been accessed all day but we aren't sure who is behind this or why as nothing has been stolen yet. Usually cyber thieves target receipts and identities but no data or money has been touched so it's quite a puzzle. Whoever they are their intrusions have caused some of the mall's attractions to break down as well as disabling some cameras and security features. Because of this we have been fixing things for hours since earlier this morning. What they are doing could be just a prank orchestrated by bored hackers, or possibly someone or something with more sinister intentions. All we have been able to do is to make repairs and continue to monitor until their purpose becomes clear."

# XVII

*S*cipio was a very flamboyant personality and his attire reflected this. He was immaculately dressed in a white silk shirt and a cravat. Like an oldtime safecracker he wore kidskin gloves to protect his hands, the tools of his trade. He topped off his look with a black cape, fedora hat and silver topped cane. His specialty was reproducing condensed versions of classic movies revamped for the puppet stage and rewritten to showcase the comedic talents of his children. In Scipio's hands Hitchcock's Psycho was a comedy. The stalker had a butcher knife, but the lady in the shower had a frying pan. The performances took place on a high-tech portable puppet stage complete with state-of-the-art lighting and sound. The diorama was painted in varying shades of gray to simulate a three dimensional scene from a black and white movie. The effect rendered the puppet strings nearly invisible, sometimes you saw them, sometimes you didn't. His goal as an artist was total invisibility.

He had arrived in this country several years before seeking artistic freedom, meaning more money and less taxes, and maybe his own television show. Back in his native Napoli there was a time when puppetry was a venerated art form and some of Scipio's predecessors had given command performances. Once as a child watching an adaptation of Romeo and Juliet in the town square, he stood in the crowd with royalty and some of Europe's finest actors and painters. A third-in-line to the throne gave him a candy apple and lifted him to his shoulders for a better view. The peasants cheered at the performance, aristocrats bowed, the priest graced him, soldiers saluted, ladies swooned. It was an epiphany for the seven year old son of the village doctor. Epiphanies are when life's lessons come together in a single awakening, all alone after a heavy night, feeling light and unconfused for the first time ever, free of selfish gravity, just you and the universe. Powerful poison. That afternoon found boy Scipio in his mother's rose garden dismantling a trellis into the sticks that would become his first marionette, a crude Scaramouche. The puppet show and it's aftermath had left him a child possessed, or so it seemed to the nuns as he danced spasmodically past the abbey as if controlled by strings.

Scipio's agent had booked him a two week stint at a shopping mall. The management felt they needed a distraction, a gimmick to give the children something to engage them while their fathers haggled over comic books. To his own amazement Scipio was a hit and the next week a doll convention was held. Same results.

Daughters watched the puppets while their mothers played with the dolls. Scipio was the toast of the tots. However his dreams of a television show never materialized. He was strictly a marionette puppeteer and usually didn't care for hand puppeteers but he idolized Shari Lewis, you know the one with Lambchop the sheep. She was pretty and most importantly she had a television show five days a week. But there was little demand for his brand of puppetry on American Tee Vee. Too sophisticated for children, too childish for adults, and teenagers just didn't get it. The main hitch was that most puppet shows aired on Saturday mornings and Saturday mornings were no good for him. It had something to do with his Friday nights. So there he was flat broke and down to his last gulp of discount wine, when an angel in disguise as his agent, trench coat, cigar, came through the door.

"Skippy baby, you're in business. Shake it off kid I got you a gig!" "A what?" "A job sweetie, a job!" "On television?" Ignoring him the agent continued "A permanent job in a shopping mall! A very big shopping mall" "Never! I have never heard of something so humiliating! I would rather work on a street corner like a Gypsy!" In fact he already had a corner picked out, plenty of shade, heavy foot traffic in front of a café just like old times in Napoli. The agent then went for Scipio's weak spot "You should think of the kiddies..." He alluded to the marionettes and went on to paint a portrait of shivery poverty. "..out there in the cold heartless streets breaking their backs for nickels and dimes, dancing in the slush like brokendown hoofers. Holes in their socks, shoes falling apart, wet clothes caked with sidewalk salt, paint flaking off, faces cracking in the icy wind. They wouldn't make it through the first winter." The agent was good at this sort of thing, enjoying it even. "Picture em Skippy, sleeping in garbage bags, bus station lockers, barefoot with swollen joints, broken strings, lockjaw!" "Enough!" The mere thought of his children in splinters brought Scipio to his senses. In the mall they could have a new stage, new trunks to sleep in, with drawers for spare parts. Just sign on the dotted line. It was a tough choice but Scipio signed. Later he reluctantly admitted to Ms. Parlett that it was best decision he ever made.

The EL lit up and started moving again past the outdoor skating rink and rows of parked buses, that were normally the other form of travel from the hotel to the mall. Reassured of his safety Scipio resumed his conversation. "I saw your Mr. Gatewood today." "He's not particularly my Mr. Gatewood." responded Chrissy. "Well he is the assistant manager isn't he?" "Unfortunately yes, but he's not much help around here." "Well he indicated to me that unless I started performing more frequently that he would be replacing me. I admit I have a teeny, tiny problem but you know I've been working on it." His problem was more than teeny or tiny but Chrissy let that go because he had recently started attending the group sessions that she had suggested he sign up for. Soothing an artist's ego was becoming all too familiar to her but she was realizing that it was a major part of her job. "He can't replace you because you are irreplaceable. You are the premier of puppeteers!" Apparently Gatewood had interfered again. His actions were definitely becoming more suspect and she was quickly coming to the conclusion that there was a lot going on that she wasn't aware of but being fair-minded she wasn't about to voice her feelings no matter how unsettling until she had all the facts. "Well you do know what day tomorrow is don't you so we can all relax, take it easy and not worry about the comments of someone who doesn't know what he is talking about." Scipio responded "Yes I love the snow, the pine trees, the mistletoe, the elves, in fact I've been seeing a lot of elves lately. They come backstage and poke around and even try on my puppet's clothes. Some of them speak Italian others French or Swiss." Chrissy made additional notes on her voice recorder. "Yes, I've been noticing an excess of elves myself. We may have over hired in the elf department, but this year has been somewhat of a trial run and we'll be able to strike a proper balance next year." Was everyone around here delusional? Elsie and now Scipio talking about elves as if they were some kind of magical creatures and not the hardworking, hard nosed little people that she had just finished negotiating with. Probably it was the season, plus too much eggnog and the general euphoria one always feels at Christmas time. "So you believe that I'm not imagining them?" he seemed relieved "but either way no matter. I love my work Christina but it is a lonely solitary life. and I welcome visitors."

"Were you ever married?" Asked Chrissy. "Yes, but my wife ran off with the owner of a laundromat. She said I was always away working and that she needed someone with a steady income which is when my problem really started. Sadly I have never found my soulmate." The snow was getting heavier now and it was almost a total whiteout outside so that the wipers and heating coils on the pod were barely making a dent. Fortunately they had arrived at the hotel and were able to disembark just as the EL shut down again.

"The party is this way, follow me Christina." prompted Scipio as they exited the EL. Parlett hesitated as she was exhausted from the day's events, gravity having definitely singled her out, even her earrings felt like they weighed a pound apiece. Her nerves were tangled like a set of last years Christmas lights but she decided that she had to show up at least for a little while especially since she had been expected to give a short speech. They entered the giant lounge marked with this sign, 'Leave Your Brain At The Door.'

# XVIII

**K**KST TV 5 had a logo. A big red 5 with a little hole in the center where someone had tossed a rock through it last fall. (Investigations were still underway.) The Station also had a jingle, which was an embarrassment to everyone except the composer who wrote it more than a decade ago. The songwriter was a former employee of Channel Five, now a minor local celeb, but still something of a poltergeist around the station, long gone but still an irritation. He had started out as a feature reporter, wrote this catchy tune on the side and signed a twenty year contract for it, then worked his way up to second anchor. However, he got demoted to weatherman and movie critic after a showdown with the management. His name was Billy Hopper and his logo were rabbits. If he liked the movie he gave it four hops. If he hated the movie the rabbits dove into a hole, and if he loved the movie he gave it his 'Golden Carrot' award, accompanied by munching sounds, his own idea.

However the rabbits were apparently agoraphobic, sticking too close to the hole and jumping in much too often. The hate mail poured in, not only from movie buffs but from network executives who had already signed deals to air the movies the rabbits found so repulsive. His dismissal was short and sweet "Thanks for the Jingle, Bye, Bye!" He did a few commercials for a local radiator shop and then his broadcasting career dove into a hole. A few years later he resurfaced in the local supper clubs. He opened with his jingle and closed with another original song 'Something to fall Back On.' Being a hit with the senior set this provided him with a reasonable living and money to cover his therapy costs. (Rumor had it that he was the rock thrower.)

The TV station owned two vans, three cars, a Limousine for any celebrities that showed up, a Jeep for fast breaking news in the boonies, and a helicopter. They all bore the big red 5, which rhymed with drive, live, and thrive, giving a idea how pretty jive the jingle was. As Chick Archer and his crew drove through the entrance gate "Any idea where we're going?" he asked hopefully. As a local features reporter his sole goal was pursuing that Big Story, the one that would put him on the map. He was a good storyteller but fate or bad scheduling always had him doing puff pieces which although entertaining were way below his abilities. Nevertheless being a professional he always filed on time. "I heard we're going back to the Zoo" said the pilot "What!" "Just kidding, just kidding" Always with the Giraffe Zoo birth that Chick had covered a few months ago. A nice local family friendly story until Lanky's mother bit him on camera and that clip was played endlessly among his colleagues to everyone's amusement. The only other time Chick had been to the Zoo was when Simba the Gorilla's mail order bride had arrived from Tanzania. Chick was the low man on the totem poll. Now he knew why the figure on the bottom always looked so grumpy. (Check any totem pole and see if it isn't true.)

Last year he had been forced to interview the writer of Christmas Kids, a book profiling children born between the twentieth of December and the fifth of January. These kids grew up having two weeks off from school each time their birthdays rolled around and the author pointed out various character traits, good and bad, that they exhibited in adulthood due to that. He had made the talk show rounds and book signings and was treated like a superstar. Always thorough, Chick had done his research and had contacted a bunch of birthday kids of all ages and their parents that fit into this category and they had no idea what he was talking about. Finally he spoke with a real shrink and unearthed that the book author did not have a psychiatry or even an psychology degree. He couldn't believe the moxie of this quack and told him that his book was pure crud and ripped a copy in two on camera reminding the camera crew of a strong-men ripping a phone book apart. Fortunately that part of the interview was edited out so the station wasn't sued and he narrowly escaped being put on waivers.

To keep Chick under control, his assignment this year was filming some pre selected Christmas themes. Marketing consultants wanting to avoid any nastiness had outlined a plan for him pre picking some selected topics. These were demographically sound and sponsor friendly. Naturally he put his own spin on them. Behold the Twelve days of Christmas:

Christmas Tree Sales report.

Carolers' contest.

Stupendous (and stupid) yard decorations.

Christmas dinner for Vegetarians (or Just the Stuffing please.)

Whacky gift ideas for the man who has everything.

What to get for the man who has nothing (or Christmas for the homeless.)

Choc-o-holic support groups.

Mayhem at the Toy store ( I saw it first.)

Mayhem at the Airport (Santa Flies but you don't. )

Waiting in line at the Turkey and Ham Store (200 people in a Blizzard waiting in line to buy meat reminiscent of the old Soviet Union.)

Chick and Mark his cameraman, a part time college student and an intern at the station, boarded the helicopter. "This doesn't have anything to do with The Hole in the Wall Gang does it? Are we heading to their most recent crime scene?" That gang of thieves had it's nickname because in their exploits, they merely blew a hole in the wall, went in, and exited with their loot. No muss no fuss. Somehow they always knew exactly where and when to blow the hole. It was suspected that they had an inside man wherever they struck but there were never any fingerprints or other clues and for almost a year they had eluded the authorities gaining an almost legendary status.

"We are going to Mesa Verde National Park" said the pilot. "Is that where the gang is hiding out? I know Mesa Verde. There's lotsa holes in lotsa walls in that park." "For the last few weeks park rangers have been seeing strange green lights in those holes." "What kind of lights? Flashlights? Flares? Guys if we were in on the gang's capture we'd make the national news feed. Get out the night Vision Equipment." "Not needed. The lights appear after dark." "What's the fastest way there?" "Just follow the little red ants." From this height the taillights of everything moving on the highway below looked like tiny ants. Ants with white eyes and red tails. "Maybe it's a publicity stunt. You know, a money making deal to draw more tourists. If there was a real story here, they would have sent someone else. Am I right?"

They landed. " Can you see anything?" "The Fog is too thick." "That's too bad. Can we go home now?" A man stepped out of the fog like Father Marin from The Exorcist.. "Welcome to Mesa Verde National Park. Mesa Verde means Green Plateau. Sir, there's no smoking in the park." (Chick's latest attempt at quitting was crumbling under the seasonal pressure.) "And who are you?" "I think my uniform speaks for itself." "Oh you must be the Park Ranger that requested our news crew?" "Yes, because various law enforcement agencies suggested that they couldn't waste valuable resources on a story that best suited your local feature news. Let me fill you in and then you can speak with the Medicine Man." "You have a Medicine man?" "This is Medicine Country! The Anasazi were the predecessors of the modern Pueblo Indians, so we contacted the tribal council and they sent someone to investigate, a Medicine man and tribal archeologist." "And what did he find out?" "He wouldn't tell me." "Why not?" "He said we wouldn't believe him, but he seems to willing to talk to a news crew." (Apparently most people will do or say anything to be on TV.)

The Medicine Man was carrying a straw broom, a rake, a shovel and a Geiger counter in a golf bag. A golf bag was easier to lug up and down the hill than a cart. "Judging from the size of the rooms, the Indians who built this place were...um...short." commented Chick. "Yes, their guide replied. "They were little people, five feet or smaller." The green lights appeared as if on cue. "What do you think is causing this phenomena since the original inhabitants are long gone?" asked Chick. "We considered Wild Turkeys but they would have to be radioactive to glow green." Then the guide lowered his voice. "It's possible that they are the babitos, the elves, the little ones, like in Irish mythology. Get within a hundred yards of the place and they disappear. They don't leave as much as a footprint behind." "Maybe it's some sort of static discharge like St Elmo's Fire?" "We thought of that too Mr. Archer, but this is high plateau country and atmospheric conditions here don't lend themselves to that and we are too far south for Northern Lights. No reflections either." " The diggings are about a hundred feet from the floor of the canyon. Any idea how they get up there?" "They jump." "Jump?" "And bounce and when they hit the floor you can see them bouncing like rubber balls all the way up and down the valley." "I guess we can also rule out visitors from outer space." Another of Chick's problems as a reporter was his inability to keep a straight face. Ignoring this the guide continued "Sometimes they are as thick as Fireflies, green ones zooming back and forth, jumping up and down. It's almost like they're ...um almost like they're .." "Almost like they're what?" " Throwing a party!"

Chick was already making up a title for this piece. He was still short two more days of Christmas and so this could be number eleven leaving him one more to go. "And there you have it. This is Chick Archer—Channel Five Nightly News"

The pilot waved them over. "The weather department forecast a lot of snow and we have many miles to go back before this snowstorm turns into a blizzard. If we leave right now we wont get caught in it." As soon as the chopper took off and moved away into the greenish fog, a glowing green light appeared, and then another. Within moments there were lights moving around in every quarter of this ancient apartment complex.

Just then bolts of lightening lit up the sky all around them and in the direction they were traveling. "Was that lightning?" asked the pilot nervously to no one in particular. "Thundersnow! Just like in a violent rainstorm there is thunder and lightning except the precipitation is snow instead of rain. It can occur with cyclones or blizzards," said Chick. "How do you know so much about the weather all of a sudden?" asked the pilot. "You never know when that knowledge might come in handy." The way the winds blew at the station Chick had been studying up about the weather just in case his next assignment was being demoted to weatherman.

As they approached their destination the pilot hovered "OK we just made it before this snowstorm got too heavy to fly through, where do you want me to drop you off?" "Set me down on that rooftop helipad," "That's Raspberry Hill Mall. It's after eleven pm, the place is closed." "What kind of reporter would I be if I let a closed door stop me. Besides I have connections." "Of course your wife is the manager there I forgot." Mark, the cameraman, snapped to attention. "I'm tagging along. You had promised to introduce me to Soozie Beals. I fell for her the first time I saw her and Madame Angelica confirmed that we should be together." "Who is Madame Angelica?" asked Chick. "A Gypsy fortune teller in the mall, and she's for real. She even has a moneyback guarantee, a total refund if her predictions don't come true. I know Soozie already from our college classes but a formal introduction would be nice, then I will be able to ask her out." added Mark. Chick made a note to explore this later thinking that even though this fortune teller was undoubtedly a fake and good luck getting a refund as she would probably be back in Transylvania by then, it might make an interesting feature story. "You got it, and bring your camera along. You can get some nice footage when the mall is empty and quiet and no one is about."

The pilot dropped them off on the roof marveling at the observation deck with viewing scopes just like at the airport. There were several rooftop restaurants, where earlier that evening patrons had front row seats to the Christmas Fireworks display. The round top of the Planetarium was visible, This wasn't just one of the world's best Planetariums giving multiple simulated tours of the heavens daily, but a real observatory on a par with the Mauna Kea Observatory in Hawaii or the Very Large Telescope in Chile which is it's actual real name and abbreviated as VLT. The Macintosh scientific foundation provided funding for this solar research as part of Raspberry Hill University (RU) winning many accolades for teaching and research. All these attractions were closed now as the helicopter moved off and the blizzard moved in.

# XIX

*A*t the **Christmas party** there was the sound of loud music, clinking glasses and muffled cheers. "Thank you everybody for a record year. Of course since we've only been open for less than a year, and there are no numbers to compare it to, no awards will be given out as nobody has worked here long enough to earn one." Accompanied to the sound of muffled chuckles Chrissy continued. "We have all been too busy to try to look busy and there will be raises in every employee's paycheck and for you store owners you will have no cam charges for two full years as you will have seen in your letters." Understandably the cheers got a little louder. She concluded with "thank you for being part of this classic experience, something you can share with your children and grandchildren. Enjoy this evening and we'll all see each other on Monday." Monday would be Boxing Day and one of the biggest sales days of the year.

Flora sat in a booth knitting as usual. She was old school and believed in personalized Christmas presents, no gift cards for her. She was knitting a turtleneck for Chrissy, a vest for Soozie and a tie for Gatewood. She knew he would never wear it but it was her way of transmitting a message to him that a manager should have more than one tie. She was of an age where she could easily retire so she was able to call him to account whenever possible with no fear of recriminations. In addition she had been friends with Elsie since their school days which is how she had obtained the secretary job. Because of this connection Macintosh valued her insights highly and often consulted her when he wanted inside info on the goings on in the office in case his presence was needed. She didn't exactly dislike Gatewood but viewed him as an immature somewhat pompous young man who needed to be taken down a peg or three whenever possible, which she did at every opportunity. Conversely she thought the world of Ms. Parlett and admired her boundless energy and work ethic.

Parlett who was quickly running out of energy, ordered her favorite, a glass of Riesling wine with a side of raspberries. Flora insisted that she try some eggnog or spiked punch instead but Parlett was already feeling a little woozy just from the atmosphere in there, a bit smoky and slightly greenish, and Flora's drink concoctions had the reputation of being over the top which could put you under the table.

Two booths over Happy Hoppy was chatting up the professional Mrs. Claus (In real life she was actually a bachelorette). He handed her the key to his heart, or the key to something.

Scipio noticed a lady in a faux fur coat sitting alone in a booth and alongside her were a pair of snowshoes. It was Elsie. "Do you mind if I join you?" asked Scipio. He took out a solid gold cigarette case and inside were gold tipped cigarettes. Elsie lit one with a farmers match that she flicked off her teeth. "Would you like another drink?" he offered. "I'd like several more" "A woman after my own heart" "Put your money away." "You're buying? I'm flattered." "They don't charge me here." Elsie responded.

A tall muscular man bearing an uncanny resemblance to a famous cleaning products icon was sitting in another booth with a group of the mall's clean up crew and maintenance men. They were still dressed in their white work overalls and jackets that had been created by a world famous fashion designer. The idea was to make them appear as super sanitary engineers maintaining the mall as if it were a cleanroom. An occasional pedestrian eyeing their lab coats had even asked them for medical advice thinking they were in that profession. They were drinking up and laughing it up and telling sixth grade style jokes such as, "What do you get when you cross a janitor with a farmer? Answer: an ammonia scented lemon. Where do sanitary engineers get their diplomas? Answer: in Sanitariums." Chrissy couldn't quite hear the next one the party was so noisy, but reflected that even her son Jody knew better jokes than those and she interrupted their revelry. "Why aren't you guys at your posts, there's a lot of cleanup needed before Monday?" Recognizing Parlett they responded. "Mr. Gatewood gave us tonight and tomorrow off, the man has a heart, he said we could complete our tasks first thing Monday morning." "I'm sure what he meant was you could take time off *after* you complete your work *before* Monday morning" replied Chrissy icily, "The mall needs to be in tip top condition for the Monday opening." Somewhat crestfallen they assured her that it would be and she moved out of hearing so she didn't have to listen to any more of their cocktail inspired juvenile humor.

Parlett approached Mr. Obujati and his date sitting in an adjacent booth. Gone were his tribal robes and ancient jewelry. He was now outfitted in business casual, looking totally normal and non threatening. He was busy downing a Harvey Wallbanger. "Hello are you enjoying the party? I thought you didn't drink?" He smiled exposing one gold tooth. "I just don't drink on the job." He leaned over. "I brought the non-smoking potion, a special blend for your husband," "And will this concoction work?" "Almost guaranteed" "Almost?" "It hasn't been tested yet so be sure to relay the results." He followed with "Why did I receive an eviction notice?" "What? All the notices I delivered were regarding next year's rental agreement." He continued, "Not only did I receive one but so did the Clovers and their candle shop. We are being told to pack up and go by the end of the week." Parlett's head cleared immediately as she read the letter that he handed her. "I know whose doing this is" she exclaimed angrily "and I assure you I will speak with Macintosh as soon as I can. I won't allow either of you to be moved out I promise."

What was Gatewood up to she wondered. It couldn't be him causing all the problems and breakdowns she had encountered today or could it? He certainly was seemingly indifferent to the core values that Macintosh espoused as a blueprint for the mall's operations. As the mall's manager the buck stopped with her. A Grand opening with some non functional features and a less than sparkling venue would be disappointing to every-one, shop keepers, customers and visitors alike. Was he hoping that the blame for all of today's malfunctions and failures would be hers? If so making her appear incompetent and not up to the challenges of her job so he could take over? She considered all these possibilities. He was the poster boy for the failings of nepotism but since he idolized his uncle, she could hardly believe he would sabotage the entire mall just to advance himself. Besides he just wasn't smart enough to coordinate all the issues from today or maybe he was and she was vastly underestimating him.

She moved over to the bar so she could safely observe the festivities that were beginning to get more unhinged. In one corner a bar brawl consisting of stroppy show people was heating up but the brawlers were all mimes, breaking invisible bottles and chairs over each other's heads and slamming each other into nonexistent walls. When it was over only a female mime was left standing who staggered over to the bar and tossed down an invisible jigger of whiskey, then ordered a real one. Across the room the ballerina from the Red Shoes pageant was soaking her feet in Pink Champagne. A partygoer asked her if she would like to dance and her response was to throw her shoes at him. In another corner was a person in a trenchcoat with a hat partly pulled down over his face obviously trying to listen in on the conversations going on around him. Parlett surmised that this was another would be sleuth attempting to lock in the whereabouts of Macintosh and half hoping that he would show up at this Christmas party. Not a chance.

Capitan Putter swaggered over to the bar and ordered a beaker of grog. The bartender didn't know what that was, so he had to punch up the bartenders guide. (Grog is watered down rum meant to mollify underpaid and abused British sailors of old. The Captain certainly qualified after having been dunked into the golf lagoon a record 35 times today.) "Here you go Cappy" "Keep 'em coming." "Aye!" A contortionist at the bar told the bartender that she would bend over backwards for another drink and she proceeded to do just that prompting the impressed barkeep to offer her several more for a repeat performance.

Parlett noticed that all the wine bottles on display were covered in dust and asked him why that was. He explained that because it made them look old he could charge more. He showed her a jar of exotic dust that he applied daily which allowed him to keep them fully dusty at all times. Tada the magician was sitting there with his assistant Presta and now they were like lovebirds, getting along famously. The arguments they had in their magic show performances were apparently just for effect. He laid his top hat on the counter and asked the bartender if he would like to see him pull a rabbit out of his hat. "Sorry, no pets allowed!!" "Well then can I buy you a drink?" Wrong thing to say because the man replied as the world's most famous bar owner once said "I never drink with customers."

With so many performers and entertainers in the lounge there was no need for a jukebox as there was a continuous spontaneous floor show in progress. Elsie had been playing the tango on the piano for groups of dancers including some of Santa's elves that had recently appeared but Chrissy didn't recognize. The next act was Evy and the Sweet Talking Snakes who we remember earlier as The Eves caroling group. They had assumed their real persona as a retro punk band and belted out a few unintelligible two minute anthems.

Seated in another corner was the browser taking in the scene. Her head and the other presents she had purchased throughout the day safely taken away to her car by the mall's complementary delivery service. She did have to wait as the valets were extremely busy and although that was somewhat irritating it was certainly better that having to traipse back and forth to do it herself. Always on the hunt for unique objects, she had started her day by visiting the *Glass Blower's Workshop.* Amazing how a few basic ingredients, mostly sand, limestone and soda ash could be turned into such rare and beautiful creations. The craftsmen attired in heavy protective gear working the molten glass in the scorching ovens reminded her of workers in a steel factory she had once visited years ago. No longer in the service of industry they had turned their talents to making art. The multicolored bowls and vases they produced seemed to shine from within and she was even given the opportunity of creating an item of her own (part of the tour). After that it was off to Wimpole place where earlier we had followed along with her adventures. Then a visit to the bookstore where she perused the shelves selecting some new reading material as she was a avid reader, followed by a light snack. Not believing in predictions for the future she nonetheless visited the Gypsy fortune teller just for the fun of it. Prediction: *You will meet a stranger. A cute little fellow. He will show you the way.*

She had arrived at the Christmas party by accident following instructions she had received at the antique shop. A short gentleman in an elf costume had handed her the directions and a jar of exotic dust assuring her that it would be well worth it. Reviewing her day's purchasing successes while drinking a slightly tart white wine she realized the she was totally enjoying herself even though she was certainly out of her element or was she. Observing these show people the browser (real name Hesper meaning evening star) was reminded of her childhood. Ballet lessons had been one year's Christmas gift and it wasn't just the dancing she loved but the camaraderie of the troupe and other performers she had met. They always seemed full of joy and even though her skills weren't enough to make a career of it the fun she remembered from those days reminded her that she definitely needed more fun in her life now and decided her new year's resolution was to do just that. Armed with the pleasant memories she now carried that had been conjured throughout the day she stopped over to thank Chrissy and assured her that she would tell all her friends and return again soon. As she left the gathering she turned around one last time and thought to herself. Yes, the little elf had been spot on, definitely worth it.

Meanwhile Scipio had raced up to his room and had returned with a puppet (real name Angelo) dressed as Fred Astaire. Elsie launched into a rendition of No strings, no connections. He had a Ginger Rogers puppet also but only two hands. In his dreams he had ten hands and could have operated them both simultaneously. In fact after so many drinks he seemed to see ten hands right now. When it was over Elsie offered "That was wonderful and I couldn't even see the strings." Scipio his heart pounding said "We make a good team. Now I can have music in my shows." The audience could see the strings but because Elsie normally wore contacts, different colors each day, her vision was a little blurry. No matter, perhaps Scipio had found his soulmate after all.

## XX

**P**arlett left the party and all the raucous behavior knowing that since the lounge was considered to be a private club the booze would be flowing until sunrise because of a loopyhole in the law. She crossed the usually busy lobby which was empty now. No bellboys or desk clerks, no businessmen settling in for the night laptops charged up for the presentations they would be writing, no beaming couples heading for the honeymoon suites. It was difficult to imagine any man taking his bride to a shopping center for a honeymoon but it was usually the new wife's idea so she could spend as much as possible before marital budgets inevitably kicked in.

She walked over to the elevators and took the one marked 'Up to Residences.' Her apartment, the manager's apartment a perk of the position, was a penthouse on the top floor. She opened her door to complete darkness, except for a flashing red light on the answering machine. Ten messages. She listened. "Sorry dear" she heard the voice of her mother. "My flight was cancelled due to the blizzard. We'll have to spend Christmas together next year." Chrissy searched the apartment. No one. She pulled out her phone and discovered that it was off. She had been getting so many robocalls earlier in the day she had turned it off and had forgotten to turn it back on. She immediately called Chick and explained "The kids, mom's not able to visit because of the storm and I left them at the mall. Meet me there as soon as you can." She ditched her costume which was now heavily scented with alcohol and cigar smoke from the party and donned more comfortable shoes and warm clothes.

Then she called Soozie hoping she hadn't gone home yet. Soozie was very dedicated and often worked late. Fortunately she was still in the office evaluating the special events she had programmed for that day and the plans for Monday and feeling very pleased with herself. She was still wearing her sugar plum fairy outfit but had removed her wings as they kept getting in the way of her typing and her headset. They arranged to meet by *The Tree* and start the search from there.

As soon as Parlett and Soozie met up and set out on their search they encountered the aquarium keeper locking up for the night. This aquarium was better referred to as a Megaquarium as it was huge!! Millions of gallons of water encased in see-through plexiglas, super reinforced and crisscrossed with many walk-thru tunnels so that visitors would be surrounded above, below and on both sides for the complete underwater experience. Parlett asked him "What are you doing here so late?" "Feeding the fish and making sure they have enough food to last until Monday morning so they don't eat each other." Two nosey dolphins pressed their noses against the glass as nurse sharks circled above them like vultures deciding if they should just wait to be fed or not. A whale went by in one great overture of protuberant overtones. She observed seahorses swaying in the sea grass including one really fat one. "That is one fat sea horse" she commented. "He's pregnant, the males carry the babies." was the response. Nature is full of great ideas thought Chrissy.

The sea floor was littered with debris, sunken ships, treasure chests and the bones of extinct marine life but no plastic. Macintosh's science foundation was working on various types of biodegradable plastic which they sometimes tested in the aquarium and so far their inventions seemed to be working. For seaside authenticity animatronic seagulls circled overhead as did animatronic flying fish. They had tried the real thing but since neither species would confine themselves to the aquarium area it had caused problems when customers complained of inopportune landings in their meal or on their new clothes. Once at Josh's Deli a customer had exclaimed.

"Waiter there's a fish in my vegetable soup." Josh in usual Catskills' fashion had responded "Don't worry, no extra charge for the protein."

Floating on top of the water were two Pirate ships and below them two submarines that usually conveyed excited customers the entire length of this mini ocean but they had to be shut down earlier that day as they had malfunctioned. (More glitches, but no one was hurt). Same with the diving bell, or bathysphere which earlier had been functioning but now had a closed sign by it's entrance.

At one end of this artificial ocean the glass overlooked a seafood restaurant, now shuttered for the evening, that allowed customers to view the fish and eat them as well just not the bioluminescent ones. At the other end was a sand beach for swimming and surfing. And trendy beachware, towels, surfboards, flippers, and the like were provided by two shops for the beachgoer, *Beachy Keen* and *Kiki of Waikiki*. There was a high diver from Acapulco brought in to thrill the crowd and also mermaids and mermen that performed aquabatics during the day but they had finished up their shows and were now enjoying the party over at the hotel. Angled off to the side was a raging river set aside for white water rafting. All was quiet now since the raging part was operated by the computer and had been shut down for the night. There was also a world renowned Scuba school and the diving teacher was underwater setting up for Monday's lessons. He noticed Ms. Parlett and held up a whiteboard "Are you lost? Do you need directions?" She held up a clipboard to the glass with these words. "Your rent is due!" He scooped some coins out of a treasure chest "Kiss my Octopus! Come and get it!" "Don't look behind you!!" wrote Chrissy on the board as the Octopus swam into view. Unbeknown to his keepers this same Octopus got around and not just in the aquarium. Tired of always being confined this Octopus had figured out how to unlock doors and often roamed the mall at night leaving puzzling wet trails for the clean up crew.

TOWARD THE END OF the day Gatewood had headed for the exits. After shorting everyone else's hours why shouldn't he knock off early also he reasoned. In the security office monitors covered a wall sixty feet by one hundred feet but almost all of the fifty monitors were dark now. Sarge spied Gatewood on one of the two CCTV cameras that were still working, and invited him into the office for what appeared to be a serious chat. "Mr. Gatewood I need your help with something. I have been receiving complaints all day about missing deliveries." and he showed him his clipboard with a rather long list. "These are all items that will be much needed by businesses to restock for Monday's shopping." "Well you should definitely take all your men and search until you get to the bottom of this." replied Gatewood as he turned to leave. "That's just it sir, you gave everyone the evening off remember? All my men is just me and two other staffers, Cooper and Angelina, so I will need you to come with us." Gatewood had tried to cut spending by giving as many of the staff as possible the evening off under the guise of giving them time off to spend with their families. Thinking quickly he responded. "Of course I'll go with you. This mall is owned by my uncle and I will be happy to help." Sarge rolled his eyes. "Let's start with the storage area then the loading dock. Perhaps these shipments were just misplaced or never unloaded, but keep in mind that nationally cargo theft adds up to billions of dollars yearly." The idea of saving billions a year really appealed to Gatewood and he immediately perked up. As they proceeded down to the storage area on the escalators which were working again the lights in the Mall went out. "Now What?" "Don't worry sir the emergency backups will kick in." And they did although now instead of brilliant light the effect was that of muted light like in a dream. Muted light with faint greenish overtones.

HIGH ABOVE JODY AND Zeeke had continued watching through the telescopes and what finally came into view was very unsettling. They observed men below who were systematically removing paintings from the mall's walls. What came next was even more surprising. After taking them down they were carefully wrapping each one in colorful wrapping paper disguising each painting as an attractive Christmas gift. All afternoon these professionally wrapped gifts had been carried through the mall by these interlopers blending in with the real delivery service. At last here was everyones answer to the puzzle. Macintosh's prized art collection was under attack. The many malfunctions earlier were designed and perpetrated to keep everyone busy fixing them to distract from the real issue that this was an art heist. Someone running this gang had put a lot of planning into this deception and it was working with perfect precision. "We need to find mom and let her know." said Jody and Zeeke agreed that it was time to get a move on. "One thing is sure, because of the storm the thieves cannot leave until morning so we should have plenty of time to carefully formulate a plan before we run out of time." "What happens if we run out of time?" asked Jody. Zeeke explained "It is the art that inspires all the artisans here and it is their creations that inspire the customers. Once the art is gone then the heart of the mall is gone and the chain is broken. Macintosh may or may not realize it but he is a magician, a weaver of dreams. We must do everything we can to protect his vision because without it there would be no more fantasy and we would go back to being a one dimensional world.

We can and will fix this, I promise!" Before they headed down to the mall floor he whispered a few instructions to his men. Jody overheard him conclude with "I'll let you know when we are ready."

As CHRISSY AND SOOZIE approached a waterfall that cascaded from the top floor to the bottom floor they saw Chick and Mark and shortly after that Jody, Kacy Jack and Zeeke appeared and joined the group. Hugging Jody and Kacy Chrissy explained "Grandma wont be arriving, her plane was cancelled due to the storm." At that point they heard footsteps behind them and turned to find Sarge and Gatewood.

Jody pointed to some empty spaces on the walls and explained that they had seen paintings being removed from their displays at several locations. Apparently the thieves had been at this for hours surreptitiously but in broad daylight, ferrying their wrapped Christmas packages down to the loading dock for transport. At that moment they saw two men in a deer suit emerge from the Art gallery carrying a large painting which they carefully wrapped and then they proceeded to heatedly argue about which color bow they should use.

XXI

**M**acintosh's **Art** collection was valued in the millions, with many paintings scattered around the mall and hotel as well as in the Art gallery itself. Chrissy quickly realized that this was no petty theft. She knew that all the pieces were secured with the latest in security tech but tonight all bets, and electronics were off. The thieves had seen to that. This appeared to be very well planned. These miscreants simply took paintings down off the walls, wrapped them in gift wrap and posed as delivery people. As the two thieves moved away Chrissy whispered "we need to follow them."

Chrissy turned her attention back to her kids. "I'm so glad you are safe but where did you get those tattoos!!" "Don't worry mom they are stick ons, just temporary from one of the many shops we visited today." Satisfied for the moment she turned her attention to Jack and Zeeke. "And just who are you people?" "Mom these are our friends, Jack and Zeeke. Jack has been giving us a tour of the mall and Zeeke is well….. I'll let him tell it."

After a brief pause. Zeeke explained. "My name is Zeeke, I am an elf originally from the mountains but now we live here in the mall." Chrissy rolled her eyes "You live here? In the mall?!" Zeeke paused "You have no reason to believe me but I promise I am here to help. We have been watching strange goings on throughout the day. You must have noticed the many mechanical outages, including the train breaking down, flooding in Wimpole place. computer glitches which resulted in cameras going off line and shipments going missing. My trusted fix it guys made repairs as fast as possible so that customers could continue to shop and that has kept my brothers very busy correcting one issue after another."

Chrissy nodded in agreement. "So it is you that have been repairing some of these issues that I thought were fixing themselves. First I thought it was coincidence, but since I did have a long list of problems from today I felt they just had to be connected in some way. I considered that perhaps this was system overload as today was our first full stress test. Then I thought that we might have a mole in the mall, but moles usually work for the competition and everyone knows that Raspberry Hill Mall has no competition!" She didn't mention her earlier suspicions of Gatewood, and although she had already dismissed the idea that he could possibly be responsible she was slightly angry at herself that for a short while, against her better judgement she had thought he was more clever than he obviously wasn't. Zeeke continued "As we now know someone is stealing Macintosh's paintings! Since they have been disguised as Christmas gifts, all the security crew would have seen is delivery people apparently doing their job. And with most of the cameras not working all would have seemed on the up and up as the thieves went about their thievery unnoticed. Genius actually."

Of course being a reporter Chick had to question Zeeke to find out who he really was. "I've read the books and seen the movies, elves are tall, slender and athletic and you are only four feet tall." In response Zeeke then related the elves' story. "We came from The Placid Mountains, a large mountain range in the big continent east of here." Chick guessed Zeeke was talking about the Alps. "Because we lived in rarified air at that high altitude, four feet is our usual height limit and many of us are even smaller. We are all relatives of a sort tracing our ancestry back to a small band of mystical elves from an even larger mountain range further east." Chick guessed he must now be referring to the Himalayas. "These ancient elves lived in huge stone igloos and wandered the enchanted grounds just above the timberline and just below the tundra where the clouds gathered and the snowflakes formed, where the wind sang in the passes, snowbirds warbled in the trees and raindrops floated down as lightly as bubbles.

This was a kingdom of exotic animals, elves and Holy men and they all thrived in this wilderness. There were very few encounters between elves and humans but the shock of an occasional meeting was accompanied by a surprised utterance of "Yikes!" which each group then understandably thought was the others' names. This misnomer continued for the longest time until they got to know each other better and for years they all lived together in complete harmony with nature."

"Then warriors appeared from the east desecrating the land and legend has it that these ancient elves moved westward looking for new homes which the Placid Mountains provided. I'm sure you are aware that most philosophies, ancient religions, mysticism and historical treatises involve mountaintop retreats. Mountains and higher elevations allowed our powers to grow." He left these powers specifically vague because although these elves had many magical powers which they always used for the good, he knew that sharing them with mortals might cause fear among the populace. It was better for all concerned to keep this information on the downlow and only use magic when absolutely necessary and as secretly as possible.

"At some point our small tribe had to move on again for even though we practiced the science of Dapatata and were virtually unseen, the location was becoming overcrowded with tourists, skiers, ice skaters, snowboarders, bobsledders and even in the warmer summer months there were hikers and sightseers riding the lifts to gawk at the beautiful mountains and catch glimpses of the glaciers before they completely receded. "What is the science of Dapatata?" asked Chrissy fascinated now by the story unfolding. After today's events so far, Chrissy was becoming more open to accepting any and all possibilities. Openmindedness often takes years of learning and unlearning, and is only experienced by those willing to toss some baggage along the trail, to clear their heads one way or another, and keep them light enough to step into unwanted territory without going mad. Zeeke explained their philosophy. "It is the ability to adapt to one's surroundings. with the least amount of effort, and the ability to blend in without drawing attention to one's self which is a prerequisite for survival when one is only three or four feet tall! "

He concluded "Many legends can be attributable to us including stories of Leprechauns, Fairies, and the Green Man. These archaic tales were invented by a few people who didn't wish to appear crazy, to explain unexplainable events when no one including themselves believed what they had seen. We next took up residence in Wales. The mountains were not so high but it was a pleasant country and if it were not for their oh so difficult language we might have stayed, so we boarded a ship and headed for a land of ice. The mountains there were breathtaking but always rumbling with fire and spewing ash. Humans seem to have adapted to this environment somehow but our usual adaptability failed us this time so again we moved on."

"After a series of adventures we ended up at Mesa Verde. There were tiny homes already constructed, albeit of cold rocks and stones reminding us a bit of our ancient origins. Since they were deserted for no apparent reason it seemed a reasonable place to stay for a while. Now however, tours of sightseers have been arriving constantly, and scientists are poking around and turning over every stone to try to solve the mystery of the original inhabitants. Once again it was time to go."

"So, you expect us to believe that it was your people we saw at Mesa Verde earlier this evening, glowing green lights and all? If this is true can you go ahead and prove it?" responded Chick realizing that true or not it could add to his nice newsworthy piece, his twelfth Christmas story perhaps. Zeeke gently removed a walking stick from beneath his coat and sighed. "What's that supposed to prove, that's just an old tree branch." Barely had Chick finished speaking than Zeeke began to glow a deep forest green until his entire person was bathed in a green glow surrounding him like an impenetrable shield. "You were saying? And by the way although short, we are slender and athletic as you can see."

"You are magic elves!" said Kacy "I knew it!" Zeeke

THE NIGHT VISITORS | 181

replaced the elf stick under his coat almost resuming his previous visage until only a faint greenish glow persisted, Now they all knew it.

"Dad" said Jody almost reading Chick's mind "This is perfect. It's the breakthrough you have been looking for. Once you air this story, you will never be back at the Zoo again." What none of them knew yet was that the elves only revealed themselves to people in the regular world many would fail to believe, children and reporters being prime examples, thus the creation of those mystical yarns.

Zeeke finished the story. "An advance party of myself and some of our band, finally discovered this perfect place. Large and very spacious, plenty of places to hide, some friendly shopkeepers, warm in winter and cool in the summer with endless varieties of cuisine. Here at Raspberry Hill Mall we make our living doing odd jobs for the tenants, furniture rearranging, computer debugging and minor repairs etc. There are a few entrepreneurs that suspect who we are and are afraid to believe it, but most are oblivious assuming we are the Santa's elves earning a little extra on the side especially since we always ask for payment in cash. We also are purveyors of our own very special recipe of exotic dust which seems to make you humans more amenable to one another among many other uses."

## XXII

**D**_own at the loading dock_ the gang ringleader spoke up. "Great job guys! The diversions we created earlier today have thrown the authorities in the mall completely off the track. We've been able to carry these paintings right past them and they had no clue as to what we were up to. This is the first time we are doing a heist without having to blow a hole in the wall and so now we may even have to change our gang's nickname!" He was so full of himself that he laughed maniacally with the assurance of someone who had lived a life bragging of his exploits no matter how nefarious. "They were so busy looking for their misplaced shipments and fixing machinery that tomorrow they won't realize that all these paintings are missing until we are long gone. With most of the cameras disabled they wont even have a record of us ever being here. In the morning when the snow stops we will just drive away and we'll all be rich even after having to fence this junk at a discounted price." Obviously he wasn't much of an art lover which was perhaps their bigger crime. Fine art doesn't have a dollar value as much as the public have always tried to put a price on it. Each piece is created once and forever can never be duplicated. It is art that uplifts us from an ordinary life to an ideal world that spans past present and future. Anyone who has stared at a *Monet* long enough, such as *The Duck Pond*, can feel themselves being drawn right in, walking down the path and morphing into a part of the panorama. Amazing to most of us, totally meaningless to him.

Ever since they had started their crime spree a year ago these thieves had become quite flush with cash from the loot they had accumulated and unloaded through the underworld. No one had come close to catching them and this overconfidence had prompted this last big heist, their hubris blinding them to the fact that it was always that one last time that historically brought many evildoers to justice. "If we are stopped and they look in the truck we will just appear to be making a final Christmas delivery to waiting customers and they will wave us through the gate unsuspecting."

This master ringleader had thought of everything, well almost everything. Readers of crime novels could have told him that no matter how clever and well planned there was always something crooks missed. *There was always the unexpected!* In this case it was the assumption that the mall would be empty at this time of night, having heard that Gatewood would be giving almost everybody the night off. A newly hired security guard they had on their payroll had filled them in on the day's schedule and the security systems in place. They had been planning this robbery ever since the mall opened waiting for bad weather to cover their tracks and a deserted mall in a blizzard seemed to make their plans even easier.

And yes, the mall would have been almost completely deserted this night had a series of coincidences not placed our heroes at the right place at the right time. Quietly our group had entered a balcony overlooking the loading dock area and were watching from behind shipping crates as the gang members stacked the wrapped paintings into a large truck which was almost full. "Mark are you getting this?" whispered Chick. "Yes and the audio too."

Chrissy took charge "Sarge, you need to call the rest of your security crew and bring them down here, there's too many of these robbers for us to just walk over and politely ask them to give themselves up. There are at least thirty of them and only nine of us not counting children." "About that." said Sarge. "Gatewood here gave the entire security crew and maintenance crews the night off. We're it, there is no one here but us!" Everyone rolled their eyes.

They watched as the two men in a deer suit returned with another exquisitely wrapped painting still arguing about the color of the ribbons. "But why would Bob and Phil lend themselves to this?" said Chrissy. "Probably because it's not Bob and Phil in the deer suit" said Jack as they watched two complete strangers climb out of the suit and one of them muttered "Next time I want to be in front." "Oh dear I hope Bob and Phil haven't come to any harm." worried Chrissy out loud. "No need to be concerned for them." said Gatewood. Chrissy rolled her eyes. "Don't tell me. You gave them the day off too!"

What was there to do now. After a few minutes Zeeke explained his idea. "Since we need reinforcements I have a plan. It will employ some traditional and possibly some more unorthodox methods. As soon as all is in readiness I'll be right back" and after whispering them the details he turned to Jody. "Follow me and bring your sister. She is a little too young to be in the skirmish that will be taking place soon" and with their parents approval off they went. Zeeke led them through an extensive series of hidden tunnels that opened up at the mall stables. "How did you know where these stables were and how to get here?" asked Jody. Zeeke replied. "I told you I knew every nook and cranny in this mall. This is one of the nooks."

The stables were located on the west side of the mall and during the warmer months opened onto a pleasant outdoor paddock where the horses could stretch their legs and nibble on fresh grass. Now of course the doors were closed up against the storm and the horses were inside cozy and warm. Zeeke pointed out a smaller horse in one of the stalls. "This one is very gentle and she will be perfect for you. Up you go." He and Jody lifted Kacy to the horse's back. Elves were simpatico to horses' feelings and though they couldn't actually talk to them their intentions were communicated in a subtle way, as they were able to do with all animals. "No matter what, you must stay here and look after this horse." Kacy was thrilled, finally her wish fulfilled.

Zeeke turned to Jody. "I need you to put bridles on a few horses and I will return with some of my people. Then when I give the signal with my elf horn you will open the doors to the mall. Women have always been better with horses and the same is true in the elf kingdom. My wife Bee will ride the lead horse and guide the rest of the herd to cause a stampede. Those thieves aren't the only ones that can cause confusion!"

Back at the loading dock Chrissy was angrily questioning Gatewood about his actions. She was definitely relieved that he wasn't the reason behind most of the problems today but there was still much to discuss and she let go on him. (It's hard to speak angrily in a whispered voice but Parlett was a pro. She and Chick rarely argued as a couple but when they did it was always in whispers so as not to wake the kids.) "What did you think you were doing dismissing everyone for the night? There's a reason we have a security team. These paintings are worth millions and more than that they are Macintosh's prized possessions! There is nothing he values more. Not to mention the replacement value of all the other merchandise in the mall. And don't think I don't know about the eviction notices. The Clovers are such a sweet couple and wait until you see the new custom candles they have created. As if you would ever spend any time at the shops, then you would actually appreciate the uniqueness of this place. You know that I should report this to Macintosh but since I hate to throw anyone under the bus, you will need to tell him yourself. If you don't give him a thorough explanation he will find out on his own anyway, so better to relate it now than later." Gatewood knew that he was in hot water and tried to put on his most contrite look without much effect. However, his takeover dreams vanishing, he was starting to realize how serious this was and was beginning to be resigned to having to face the music even if the result was that his Uncle might actually disown him. Not to mention that the manager's penthouse apartment that he coveted would be forever beyond his reach.

# XXIII

*Z*eeke soon returned with numerous elf buddies carrying sheets of Bomb Bread, the big explosion kind. They had many other pastries and also trays of pies from *The Uppercrust*, crème pies, fruit pies, pumpkin pies loaded with whipped cream, meringue pies. With them were a group of their wives armed with pots, pans, rolling pins and other utensils from the *Kitchen Stuff* store (on the sixteenth floor.) They were attached to bungee cords and ready to pounce. Vats of cool creamy liquid chocolate and buckets of honey from the *B Store* (7th floor) were quietly positioned above the crooks heads. The preparations were complete. "This would be the perfect time for a battle cry but since we aren't usually warlike and don't have one I can only say ready, go!" and he blew the elf horn as the signal to attack.

All together they descended on the unsuspecting thieves, with myriad explosions from the Bomba causing bread chunks to go flying everywhere. Streams of chocolate and honey rained down on them much like boiling oil at sieges in the middle ages. The thieves became totally disoriented and panicked as a group of glowing green elves started to pursue them brandishing elf sticks and makeshift kitchen weapons. They vowed that next time they did a heist they wouldn't consume all the cocktails and wine coolers they had during the day since that must be what was causing these hallucinations. They ran upstairs sticking to the floor tripping as they ran out through the mall, with everyone in pursuit throwing cakes and pies. Galloping horses cut them off and barking dogs in a giant pack nipped at their heels. The dogs were newly released by Sarge from the snoozing dogcatcher's van who swore that he was just resting his eyes for a moment.

The Zamboni, now operated by a real elf coated the floors with new ice and the thieves slipped and slided into each other. The cover of the round stage opened and the fountain beneath started spewing forth multicolored water from the floor to the distant ceiling accompanied by the Blue Danube Waltz. The tune was sped up because apparently these elves had the ability to speed up time or slow it down at will and if you speed up a waltz it sounds appropriately more like a cavalry charge.

These hapless thieves had no defenses against this time distortion power regardless of whatever physical fight training they may have had in the past. Slow, fast, slow, fast, slow, fast. If they ran forward they actually moved backward and if they threw a punch they ended up punching themselves and each other. Their heads were spinning and their new vow was that they would never ever steal anything ever again if they just could get through this in one piece.

Forks of lightening flashed down from *The Tree* as if some mad scientist had opened the door to his hidden laboratory. From her computer cave Mimi had been watching the unfolding events and summoning up all the volts she could muster she unleashed them on the malcreants below like an angry Zeus bringing his irreverent subjects back into line. *The Pastry Express* train came careening through the halls with elves on the carriages throwing snowballs with amazing accuracy learned from years in the snowy mountains completing the rout. After this trouncing the disheartened shaking shivering crooks were each bound and gagged with biodegradable bubble wrap and twine and treated to a frosted seat on the train, all soaking wet and some of them with meringue still on their faces. (There's nothing like a good old pie fight and ironically these were the some of the same pies from the bogus order the thieves had placed earlier meaning that their stunt had backfired in a way they couldn't possibly have anticipated.)

Separated from the main group the gang ring leader and his second in command had spied the half open door to the aquarium and ignoring the closed sign, as they never ever followed any rules anyway, decided to hide in the bathysphere. Inside there was room for a couple of would be aquanauts to walk around, enjoy the plush interior straight out of Jules Verne, (all of his inventions had plush interiors) and peer through the four viewports covered in extra thick glass. However since the elves had repaired it earlier, it was now working again and automatically started to descend lowering to the bottom as the water pressure increased. Tentacles appeared as the bored Octopus surrounded the diving bell blocking any hope of their retreat.

CHRISSY SURVEYED THE SCENE her head in her hands. One word for it. The mall was trashed! Macintosh's precious Tree was now on it's side no longer looking fresh and crisp as if it was from the winterlands but drooping like a willow on the verge of tears. (Fortunately it was insured). Some of the branches had crashed through Santa's village and if he was here to see this now she would never hear the end of it. He wouldn't ask, he would demand to be relocated and he wouldn't take no for an answer no matter how she might try to flatter him. Decorations were crushed and ripped down and there was water, half frozen ice and crumbs everywhere. Horses and dogs roamed free barking stomping and whinnying. Flocks of birds circled and chirped diving for the tasty crumbs. The mall seemed irreparable before Monday. The Grand Opening would be a hopeless disaster. It seemed that there was nothing that could repair the damage done.

But there was. "Don't despair Ms. Parlett, my people will get this cleaned up in a jiffy. Green Power will prevail! After all we have magic on our side" he winked "… and hard work." Zeeke and Bee smiled at Chrissy reassuring her. (Interestingly when you say the names Zeeke and Bee you cannot help but adjust your face into a smile.) "If you can fix this I won't know how to thank you enough "said Chrissy hoping that what they said could be true. "My pleasure," laughed Zeeke, "actually I haven't had this much fun in years. Just the expressions on their faces when we confronted them make it all worthwhile and will make a great adventure to relate by the fire on some future snowy evening." Now Chrissy laughed and realized that the ability to laugh, no matter what the occurrence, was the elves greatest power because it was one that everyone can share.

Mark had recorded everything on film and was excitedly explaining to Chick and Soozie that they had enough footage to command national, no, worldwide attention. Zeeke stepped in and addressed our little band of warriors. "You must delete or edit out any footage of the elves. If we are revealed it will cause the end of our secret existence and by extension the end of us." he related seriously. "Or more likely" he chuckled "viewers will think your story is a fake. No one will believe that you didn't doctor the footage adding elves as a Christmas publicity stunt."

"But even if we delete the elves' footage won't the criminals testify to what they had seen?" asked Soozie. Chick got it. "During my years of reporting I have observed that people rarely believe criminals, because many of them declare that they are totally innocent especially when their crimes are captured on video. They want us to believe that we didn't see what we saw even though we saw it. Now it is possible that someone will make up a conspiracy theory as they often do, but without visual evidence of the elves it will just be speculation. And think about it, would the general public or a law court believe there are actual elves living here? I'm not sure if I believe it. I do now, we all do, but it still seems fantastical. Besides we have enough footage of the crime and capture itself to make excellent reporting regardless. We'll edit out the elves and stick to our story. Are we all agreed?" One by one from Sarge to his two man crew they agreed. "But what about the reward for the gangs' capture?" asked Gatewood hopefully. "We'll donate it to charity." Said Chrissy rolling her eyes. "Besides your uncle will make sure you get your reward for leaving the mall unprotected if he finds out you had sent the security team home tonight." "What elves!" said Gatewood quietly knowing he had no choice now but to agree or become a total pariah. Besides he knew how to respond to her implied blackmail. If he didn't tell all to his uncle she most definitely would.

Mark spoke up. "I'll agree if Soozie agrees to go on a date with me". Soozie smiled "I agree and would have gone on a date with you anyway. Why did it take you so long to ask me out? Didn't Madame Angelica tell you that we were meant to be together?" "You told her to say that?" said Mark realizing that he had been hoodwinked. "I gave her a discount on the rent" she smiled, "but don't ask her for a refund because regardless it is true isn't it? Don't some things work out in mysterious ways?"

Within a couple of hours the police arrived having driven in by snow plows and snow cats and loaded up the gang removing each one from their cupcake perches. Then they slowly brought up the diving bell and handcuffed the two occupants who seemed to be suffering from a mild case of the bends. "What are they mumbling about?" "Something about Elvis!"

# XXIV

**B**oxing Day was on Monday. This holiday is traditionally celebrated the day after Christmas Day, when servants and tradespeople would receive gifts, known as a Christmas box, from their employers mostly in the United Kingdom and other English Commonwealth countries. Worldwide it has morphed into a huge shopping day when stores would discount their merchandise to move it out in preparation for incoming spring merchandise in the next few weeks. Today there were free giveaways from every store for every shopper as an enticement.

Later, since it was also the mall's Grand Opening Day, dignitaries from all over the world be arriving. Soon there would be a swarm of helicopters circling to land like angry hornets, discharging their passengers for the Blacktie event to be held in the central court. The ladies would be in gowns rivaling the couture of the Met Gala, the men would be tuxed up and sleuths looking for Macintosh were expecting him and his cortege to be in attendance. Finally they would get him on camera and get that interview.

Not a scintilla of the previous mayhem was left and since the cleanup had been done mostly by the elves it had been completed in an impossibly short time. All the horses were back in their stables happily munching on a special rasher of oats. In earlier centuries Boxing Day was celebrated by fox hunts held in many communities, but now the foxes of the world could go about their fox lives safely as that cruel sport had been abolished and so in these more civilized times horses had the day off.

Sarge and his security crew had rounded up all the stray dogs with the dog catcher's help and set up a dog adoption zone. He theorized that with the thousands of visitors to the mall daily it shouldn't be difficult to find homes for the 229 pooches they had captured. Especially now since Flora, Elsie and Bella and her staff from the pet store had washed brushed and trimmed each one completing their squeaky clean looks with shiny new collars. This program was to become a permanent feature in the mall expanding to cover all varieties of abandoned pets. As expected cats didn't take to the bathing feature with much enthusiasm but it was better than being homeless.

So the mall was now spotless and filled with happy shoppers as a small select group of employees filed into the private staff meeting that Macintosh had announced. He opened the impromptu gathering by congratulating everyone present on a very productive season and then he singled out Zeeke "I have been told that it was you and your people that are mainly responsible for this miraculous cleanup and for thwarting the gang that had their sights set on stealing the most valuable paintings in my collection. Because of my financial wherewithal I am in the position of being able to provide any reward that you may ask for." Zeeke smiled. "What I ask, you might not wish to provide." Now Macintosh smiled. He knew he could cover any request. "Name your amount."

"I would like your permission for my band of elves to live in the mall permanently. We tire of wandering the world and we feel a kinship with this place. The minute we set foot on the hill we could feel the inherent magic it exuded and I promise you wont even know we are here." Macintosh who had been expecting a dollar amount, pondered this and replied. "I rarely have time to visit here so I must leave this decision to those of you directly involved on a daily basis." (Actually Macintosh visited at least twice a week because this was his favorite project, but always in many unrecognizable disguises chuckling to himself as the would be sleuths looking for an interview often sat right across from him having a morning coffee.)

What was the most important was that Macintosh believed in participatory management and he wanted to be sure everyone was on board for this important decision. "I would like to add that if we are in agreement there is a very large annex in the attic next to Elsie's penthouse that was set aside for luxury apartments to be constructed at a later time. I could have the entire space built out to their specifications giving the elves their own secret village." This would be the best solution he decided as Elsie would have neighbors and friends right next door. He also knew that this is where the elves had already been living, as nothing ever got past him, so they may as well be more comfortable. Their computer skills could definitely come in handy if there was ever another attempted breach in the future. He had full confidence in the current system but recognized that it needed an upgrade assisted by these amazing multitalented beings. Besides he had no need for the revenue from additional apartment rentals since he was already one of the world's wealthiest entrepreneurs.

Sarge went first. "We now know that Zeeke and his friends have been living here for the past several months and neither I nor anyone on my staff have ever detected their presence. If they could lend those talents to quietly assist our security team I would consider it an honor."

Flora gave a thumbs up and Elsie seconded that and added "Their people seem to have an unnatural penchant for taking care of plants. We have the best maintenance staff in the world but with so much greenery to care for, additional green thumbs would be a valuable asset." Soozie, already thinking about the upcoming year responded "It was an amazingly speedy cleanup and if they could coordinate and help with setting up events as quickly as they repaired all the damage, I vote yes."

Gatewood piped up "Whatever you decide it's fine with me since you are my uncle and always decide for the best." Macintosh rolled his eyes. "Speaking of deciding for the best it has come to my attention that a few stores were scheduled to be evicted in the new year but there is no need for that. I am very pleased with the variety and quality of our current offerings and no changes will be made to our mix. Letters have already gone out to those shops affected reassuring them that their leases are permanent and they may stay as long as they like. I've also heard that both impacted stores have had to hire on more helpers as they are now flourishing." Now Gatewood rolled his eyes and braced himself for the recriminations for his actions that were sure to follow. "Ms. Parlett, Your vote?" "Yes of course!" She smiled. "It is decided. Welcome!" Zeeke was nowhere to be seen, already keeping his promise.

Macintosh continued. "I have another important

announcement to make. I've had a lot of requests to expand our sports footprint at the mall and I am embarking on a new addition of a full eighteen hole course complete with an expanded Golf Pro Shop. Next to it we will build a baseball park and multi use arena for sports events and concerts. There will be an archery range, a fishing pond, a hunting dog training area as well as virtual versions of all major sports from football to canoeing to duck calling. This will be a very large and challenging project covering multiple floors and acreage we will be following the LEED guidelines in the construction process, and will feature artificial lawns to minimize water use. In addition electricity will be provided by solar panels similar to the ones already here at the mall and all lighting will be Led. I will oversee this project and Gatewood you will be the onsite manager. To provide you with the time necessary for this undertaking all your other mall duties will be handled by Ms. Parlett going forward." Gatewood was so visibly thrilled at his new golf related assignment and his narrow escape from his deserved punishment that he failed to notice the alternative sighs of relief, applause and the rolling eyes of the rest of the staff.

Macintosh had finally admitted to himself that Gatewood's attempted undermining of the mall's vision of uniqueness meant only one thing. His nephew was incompetent and a bit of a weasel! However, he was his nephew after all. Right now he was young and inexperienced but everyone has to grow up sometime. This new project should keep him so busy that perhaps at some point, with actual hard work and supervision he would be salvageable.

As everyone left the meeting, he had a few last private words for Chrissy. "You can be most proud of your work here. I certainly am and I'm giving you a bonus. It should just about cover the cost of that little electric car you seem so fond of. By the way your suggestion on how to handle my nephew was perfect. Did you see how his eyes lit up when golf was mentioned! I'll have Flora continue to keep an eye on him and I'm hoping he'll amount to something eventually." Chrissy nodded but privately she wasn't totally convinced. He continued "I know you are not totally convinced but we'll see." Chrissy grinned "Thanks again for the car. Hopkins will be happy. Clever salesman. He was right to encourage the test drive because the car sold itself!"

"One more thing Chrissy, this evening when you attend the gala as my representative please be sure to thank the public for their support and give them my well wishes. They will ask about my whereabouts so just tell them I'm out of the country researching new acquisitions. That ought to send those investigative reporters scurrying in all directions to find out my possible location." Macintosh was starting to enjoy this cat and mouse game that they had started and he was ready for another round. "As always I'll be in attendance somewhere in the crowd gathering impromptu reactions and comments which as you know are usually much more reliable than formal surveys."

Finally for my part the mall is operating just the way I envisioned and you should know that my paintings are still safe and secure at my home gallery. After studying the Gardner heist, the Van Gogh heist and other famous art thefts, I had realized how difficult it would be to protect items of this value in the mall even with our advanced security since it is such a high traffic area. The many works I have on public display here that the thieves tried to steal were just excellent copies that I had paid a renowned forger to make of my originals so that all shoppers could enjoy and appreciate them. Plus with the retainer I provided him it will keep him off the streets and on the straight and narrow for a long time into the future." "You mean...?" "Correct, the originals were never on site at the mall and so never in any danger. But that will be our best kept secret, ears only." They shook on it. "But wont that affect the outcome of their trial?" "Don't forget their attempted robbery here is only one of numerous other robberies they actually committed. Ours is just a footnote to their long list of crimes." he reassured her.

Macintosh picked up a velvet wrapped box and headed

toward an exit secreted behind a bookcase. This led to hidden stairs to the private helipad which he routinely used in order to avoid the ever persistent sleuths hot on his trail. Because of what day it was they had believed that this time they would corner him. Not a chance. "What's in the box?" asked Chrissy thinking it looked strikingly familiar. "Just a belated present for the family. You know I have millions of dollars worth of art but I visited the candle shop today and this artifact is more valuable because it is a unique item created by artisans right here under our own roof!"

Parlett left the office to find Chick, Jody, Kacy, and Jack Dawkins waiting patiently under two giant palm trees. They all took turns congratulating her success and also congratulating Chick who had been promoted to anchorman at the TV station, tie optional. Kacy whispered in Chrissy's ear. "Remember my Christmas wish?" For a horseback ride?" asked Chrissy. "I had a horseback ride. The other wish." Chrissy then whispered in Chick's ear. " I approve" he said puzzled at first then a big smile. Chrissy turned to Jack. "Kacy wished for a new brother for Christmas. How would you like to live with us as part of our family, and perhaps later, only if you like the idea and agree, we could adopt you?" Jack had always considered himself to be self sufficient, his own man even at his young age, free and independent, but this was too good to refuse. A real home with some of the nicest people he had ever met, a real school and new friends to meet. "As long as I can continue to visit Elsie, Zeeke, and my other friends here." Kacy and Jody both chimed in "As long as we can accompany you, as they are our friends now as well." "Great!" said Chick. "And now there's only one more thing left to do and our Christmas will be complete. Lets go." And with that they headed off to the dog adoption area to make their selection.

*** *fin* ***

# Postscript

The Hole In The Wall gang leader is realizing the error of his ways and is spending much of his prison stretch doing art therapy. His paintings are surprisingly not that bad.

The two men in the deer suit (not Bob and Phil) have set up a prison gift service. They help select gifts for their fellow inmates and wrap them and have them shipped for delivery. They still argue over the color schemes of paper and ribbons.

McIntosh has discovered a new vein of gold at the M mines and has vastly increased his charitable giving.

The little Archer family is living happily ever after.

No one knows what the elves are currently up to as they continue to keep a low profile.

*Hope you enjoyed reading this book,*
*if so please submit a review.*